HAROLD'S YEARS
Impressions from the
New Statesman and the *Spectator*

Edited by KINGSLEY AMIS

QUARTET BOOKS LONDON MELBOURNE NEW YORK

THE SECOND PREMIERSHIP

INTRODUCTION

The time has not yet come when it is safe to say what were the really important issues and events of the Harold Wilson era, or even whether those grubby eleven-odd years will seem worth calling anybody's era, but when that time does come we shall most of us be dead and the rest of us wishing we were, so it seems fair to push on with what may be a bit unsafe to say. First, though, a personal note or two; here at least I should be relatively immune to contradiction.

When October 1964 came along I voted Labour. Of course I did. I always had done, locally as well as nationally, since 1945; the Tories were – I saw them as – the party of Suez and of expense-account living; the new man Wilson was supposed to be rather of the Hugh Gaitskell persuasion, and I had admired Gaitskell. As this implies, although he had been party leader for twenty months, Mr Wilson himself was then very little known to the general public, far less well than Margaret Thatcher had become after the same interval (i.e. by October 1976).

Once in office, however, the new man made himself known with a speed and depth that has only one parallel in our time, the advent of Edward Heath on the national consciousness in 1970. With all their differences of fortune and temperament, they are two of a kind, like a pair of linked characters in the Anthony Powell novels. But to go on – a closer look at the Prime Minister and at his colleagues, who seemed a different species from Attlee's men, disturbed me: I personally encountered the unacceptable face (and voice) of Anthony Wedgwood Benn a little later. In particular I deplored Labour's education policies, a topic which deserves a few sentences to itself.

I had left academic life in 1963, but continued to watch it closely. It was in this sphere that I had first had reason to dispute the progressive consensus I had grown up with, very likely because it was the sphere within which I myself moved (to quote Robert Conquest's celebrated Law: Everybody is reactionary on subjects he knows about). By 1952 – see *Lucky Jim*, pp. 173–4 – the modest post-war expansion of our universities had already begun to cause the lowering of academic standards which continued and accelerated for years afterwards; perhaps it now has no further to go. For me, Harold's Years were marked as much as anything by the decline of British education in school and college alike, the product partly of sentimental mercy upon the not so bright, partly of positive hostility to excellence. (The Heath government, in the person of Mrs Thatcher at the Ministry, hardly did so much as slow the rate of damage, but the times were unfavourable. The pendulum may swing back in the end, if it doesn't turn out to be a ratchet instead.)

Mr Wilson, at any rate, took no visible notice of any of this. Undeterred by the withdrawal of my support at the 1966 election, he marched on to the end of the decade, or rather sat on in his armchair, frowning at his pipe, anxious that the record be set completely straight, only too willing to share his knowledge of the overlooked and yet obvious factors that proved him right, scrupulously fair – if sometimes genially condescending – to those who were wrong. And why not? There was no one in his party to challenge him, the economy was still miraculously holding together (a lot of people were even getting richer for the moment), and something was sure to turn up.

Something did: Mr Heath, winning the 1970 election on his own. He looked formidable enough for the first year and a bit, but then showed himself to be, like his predecessor and eventual supplanter, restless, unfixed in principles and place, resolved to ruin or to rule the state – more accurately, to really ruin and to seem to rule it. Either he wasn't as clever as Mr Wilson or the economy stopped holding together (or both); certainly people stopped getting richer and Heath could be pushed out, out of Number 10 in March '74, though he clung on with his fingernails, and, to teach him, in effect out of the Tory leadership in the October. Then, in March '76, at the first plausible occasion, the Garter and retirement for H. Wilson, whom time is now carrying further every day from responsibility for whatever vast unexploded 'dirty' bomb he has left us.

The effects of those bombs whose detonation he sometimes accomplished, but more often failed or could not be bothered to prevent, are all around us. The most far-reaching of these is our joining the EEC, but to me personally, since I was born in the place and lived in or near it almost throughout that period, and still do, the most immediate is the condition of London. A trip on the top of a bus from one end of the city to another is instructive. Yes, to answer an earlier question, they were Harold's Years indeed. The Heath interregnum seems too short and too much like what went before and after to be worth distinguishing from them.

It must be said that a captain is not often unrecognisably better than his team, and that the two teams concerned, having started off in 1964 as not so good, had by Garter-day become the worst in living memory, or so it then seemed. As, partly but not largely for external reasons, the nation declined, the young men and women who a generation earlier would have gone into politics went into corporations where there was still some power left, or abroad. One of Mr Wilson's more lasting achievements will have been to see to it that most of those who would have been our leaders in twenty-five years' time are now at school outside these shores.

Of the man himself I know very little, just enough to guess that he would be fun to have a couple of drinks with, perhaps no more, though even that is saying something when you look at the competition. For the rest, I must go by what I see and hear, and what I then find I regard most of all with incredulity. How could such a man – not so much small or mediocre as insubstantial, two-dimensional like a character in fiction far inferior to Anthony Powell's – have been where he was all that time? (Here, once again, he is joined with Mr Heath.) This must be why the United Kingdom of Harold's Years, considered as a nation under 'governance', already strikes me when I look back on it as quite unreal.

What may help me and others, if not to make sense of that period, then at least to play over again some of its characteristic themes, is the continued existence throughout it of the *New Statesman* and the *Spectator*. Anyone who needs to be told what these are will hardly have read as far as this, so I need say little more than that they have no parallel that I know of in the English-speaking world, that most of the leading writers of our day have contributed to one or the other (and quite a few to both), and that their range of approach, from straight politics by way of social or personal commentary to literature, the arts and entertainment, makes them a valuable quarry for anyone in search of the nuances and overtones, as well as the major currents, of a historical period. Their respective positions to left and right of centre – though each has always been markedly hospitable to views it opposes editorially – make them usefully complementary, as do their respective styles, the *Statesman* being by tradition the brighter and sillier of the two.

According to my unrigorous computation, the contents of the two journals over the years in question amount to something in excess of 60 million words; I have not read every one. My task involved reducing this to about a thousandth of the total, and the reader will appreciate that in the process a great deal had to be left out. Since the unifying factor in the collection was the presence of a political leader, political matters naturally took priority. I had hoped to give due prominence to what has deservedly given both papers a large part of their reputation and readership, the book pages, but I found quite soon that any attempt to do so within the required length would have eaten intolerable holes in the coverage of what must be of more general concern: when the choice of topics is devolution or Drabble, it has to be Margaret who gets chopped. Reviews, then, along with arts notices and such, I have confined almost entirely to those which illuminate the wider issues.

Deciding among these – what were or what seemed to be wider issues – was no simple operation either. The United Kingdom's entry into the European Community was the only one which unequivocally demanded inclusion, just as it is the only one to have become more rather than less important in retrospect; it now shows itself to be of much the same magnitude as a British surrender in 1940 would be. As I write, the public seems to be waking up to this, but it would not be 'safe to say' whether the mood could ever give rise to a movement. With all other topics, from abortion and Berlin to youth and Zanzibar, I felt I could afford to be more arbitrary, allowing myself to be influenced by questions of balance, unexpectedness and literary merit.

Any editor, whether of an anthology or of a journal, had better admit that what he produces is only as good as his writers; I had a splendid field to choose from. But the requirements of that choice brought special disappointments: one good piece had to be dropped because it overlapped something else, another because it was founded on some now-forgotten episode, a third because it was so long that it either must be cut – an impertinence – or would leave no room for a fourth. My apologies to those contributors who are not represented as they might have wished, and to those who for this reason or that couldn't be represented at all. My thanks to everybody concerned for providing me with so many hours of enjoyable reading and re-reading; not getting sidetracked demanded constant vigilance. And my salutes to the memory of those who, to the general sorrow, are no longer able to receive thanks: Kenneth Allsop, Denis Brogan, Francis Hope, Kingsley Martin, Tibor Szamuely.

I must also express my gratitude to the editorial staffs of both journals for their generous assistance and hospitality, and in partccular to Gillian Wilce and Angela Harding of the *New Statesman*, and to

Ginny Naipaul and Lorraine Philip of the *Spectator*, for much cheerful and efficient help.

KINGSLEY AMIS

May 1977

THE FIRST PREMIERSHIP

New Statesman, 6 October 1964   Malcolm Muggeridge
THIRTEEN YEARS SOFT

Looking back on 13 years of Conservative rule, now, as we must all hope, drawing to its close, and on the men – Churchill, Eden, Macmillan, Home – who have ruled over us since October 1951, there is little that is memorable in the record, except the Suez fiasco and the Profumo scandal; two episodes which they, certainly, would prefer should be forgotten. How, one wonders, did they employ their time?

Baldwin used to disconcert the more earnest among his supporters by sitting for hours and hours on the government front bench, apparently dozing or turning over the pages of a magazine. Churchill's mental powers were already seriously impaired when he came to form his postwar government. In conversation, one of his visitors told me, he was liable to confuse the 1939–45 war with the 1914–18 one. Macmillan, one gathers, was always surprisingly available. Visitors would find him sitting ruminatively before an empty desk. Certainly, he never lacked time for one of those meandering historical disquisitions which so tried the patience of his colleagues, and reduced Americans to a condition of frenzied boredom. (Thus Kennedy, at the Bermuda Conference, in desperation was reduced to passing a note to one of his aides, telling him at all costs to intercept Macmillan's relentless flow.) Even Home, who as far as paperwork is concerned is what French schoolmasters call a *retardataire*, has been able to absent himself from Downing Street for a good proportion of his short period of office without, apparently, suffering any ill consequences. There seems to have been no particular need for him.

Few can have supposed, when Churchill formed his 1951 government, that it represented anything but a transient arrangement. The majority was tenuous; the names of the ministers, as they were announced in little batches, were far from reassuring, especially when it became clear that Churchill was hankering after a revival of his wartime overlord arrangement, with outsiders like Lord Leathers supervising the work of the regular politicians. Stories abounded of how incomprehensible appointments were made (for instance, Manningham-Buller's as Solicitor-General) because Churchill forgot faces and muddled up names. Men called to Downing Street found themselves addressed as someone else, and some, though they served in his ministry, never did succeed in establishing in the mind of the Prime Minister who they actually were.

Both in the manner of its formation and in its conduct of affairs, this government was a shambles such as has rarely, if ever, existed before. It has largely escaped criticism because of the Churchill legend. Like an Anglican clergyman turning to the altar and intoning: 'Now to God the Father . . .' on completion of his sermon, it is part of the Conservative ritual to proclaim at some point in a discourse that Churchill is the greatest living Englishman. If he is the greatest living Englishman, clearly he cannot, on the record of his postwar administration, have been one of the worst of modern Prime Ministers.

After the war, the Conservatives were stuck with Churchill, and in private groaned over the weight of the burden. They never liked him, and when he led them to overwhelming defeat in 1945 their dislike and distrust, submerged in the war years under mountains of sycophancy and adulation, came to the surface again. As Leader of the Opposition he gave them little joy. In the only private conversation I ever had with Eden, in 1951, he remarked bitterly that Churchill might yet keep Labour in office a little longer.

For the Conservatives, getting Churchill out once he had formed his postwar government was a major operation. He wanted at all costs to go on having the diversion of his dispatch boxes – his toys, as he called them. The Conservative party-machinemen, however ardently they longed for him to go, could not admit as much in public. The choicest and largest collection of abusive communications I received when I was editor of *Punch* was as a result of a cartoon suggesting that Churchill was unfit to go on being Prime Minister – a proposition taken for granted in the conversation of most of his colleagues, as well as at most Conservative dinner-tables.

In assiduously hanging on, Churchill was helped by the fact that his chosen successor was Eden, who was disliked by quite a few Conservatives and despised by many more. This may have been why Churchill was so strong for Eden to be accepted as his successor, even though, in private, he seldom troubled to hide his poor opinion of him. He may well have calculated that, if the alternative to him was Eden, he might reasonably expect to remain in office for the maximum possible time; no one was going to turn him out to put Eden in. If this was his calculation, it proved in the end mistaken. Eden, then in possession of his faculties such as they were, was preferred to Churchill with his in disarray. In the end, Churchill was told in the bluntest and most brutal terms that he had to go. In the context of British politics, it must almost have been like getting rid of Stalin. Nor would it surprise me if, as with Stalin, a mood of de-Churchillisation of the Conservative Party were, in due course, to set in. Indeed, there are signs of it already.

At long last Eden's moment came, and he moved into Downing Street, the previous incumbent having been given a big send-off on the occasion of his 80th birthday. It must be maddening for Eden today to reflect that if, instead of embarking on his fatuous Suez adventure, he had followed the normal Conservative routine and just done nothing about anything, he would probably be Prime Minister today and about to go to the country for yet another renewal of his mandate.

Precisely why he should not have run true to form is still a matter of dispute. I suspect myself that the basic reason was a desire to demonstrate that, contrary to the prevailing opinion, he too, could be a man of destiny – like Churchill, send for his chiefs-of-staff in the middle of the night, study maps, initiate campaigns, and even on occasion defy the White House. Descriptions I have heard of his conduct of the dismal affair of Suez convey an impression of a grisly parody of Churchillian war leadership; of a benzadrine Napoleon and pinchbeck Foreign Office Machiavelli all in one.

Alas, the poor fellow was ill-suited for such desperate courses, and, if a recent work (*Dulles Over Suez* by Professor Herman Finer) is to be believed, burst into a flood of weeping when President Eisenhower rebuked him on the transatlantic telephone. In a matter of months he succeeded in reducing his country to a laughing-stock throughout the world, his government to impotence, his party to confusion, and himself to a condition of nervous prostration, accentuated by excessive doses of sedatives, pep-pills and John Foster Dulles.

The lesson was not lost on his successor, Harold Macmillan. No Conservative Prime Minister, it is safe to predict, will ever again act in defiance of an American President or Secretary of State, or even of the CIA. Nor will one ever again recommend large-scale military operations in defence of imperial interests or positions. To guard against any such possibility the empire has been dismantled. 'I was not appointed to be His Majesty's principal Secretary of State,' Churchill remarked in one of his grandiloquent moods, 'to preside over the dissolution of his empire.' This, had he but known it, was precisely what he had been appointed for. Conservative ladies still sing 'Land of Hope and Glory' at their rallies, without, I should suppose, reflecting that under successive Conservative governments our bounds have been set narrower still and narrower.

Macmillan's choice came as a surprise. Churchill, for some impish reason of his own, or perhaps mistaking Macmillan for Sir John Anderson, sent him first to the Ministry of Housing. One saw him in those days disconsolate in gumboots. Nonetheless, with the expert assistance of Mr Marples, houses were duly built – at a price. Eden, to keep him away from the Foreign Office, sent him to the Treasury. There, initially, he was an ardent supporter of the Suez operation, though subsequently, according to Randolph Churchill's account, one of the decisive voices in calling it off.

After the Suez debauch, Macmillan was a sorely needed prairie oyster. The Conservatives swallowed him, and lo! their shakes subsided, their eyeballs again fitted into the sockets, and those pink elephants which Eden had summoned up mercifully disappeared from view. Telling the Wogs where they got off was all very well at garden fetes, or at meetings in country schoolrooms across a table adorned with a Union Jack; but for Eden – of all people – to carry matters to the point of actually moving troops about! And then petrol-rationing! And the pound shaky! That would not do at all. What a relief, when Eden mercifully disappeared into the shadows, to be confronted by this genial Scottish publisher, with crofter origins and ducal connections and enough relatives in and around parliament to form a family government, down to the under-secretaries!

Eden had ruled out the field of battle as a sphere of operations for Conservative Prime Ministers, but there remained diplomacy. It was in pursuit of distinction in this field that Macmillan put on his white fur hat and undertook his hilarious visit to Mr Krushchev in Moscow. No one who accompanied him (as I did) is likely to forget the experience; particularly the visit to a collective farm, with Macmillan in a grouse-moor outfit which he had brought with him for such outdoor occasions; and his speech at Kiev, when he recalled how in the 12th century a Ukrainian princess had married into our English royal family, and was not this a happy augury for relations between our two peoples?

With the collapse of the subsequent Summit Conference in Paris, Macmillan had one more try; this time to get into the Common Market. It, too, was a failure, thanks to De Gaulle, who had old scores to settle, dating back to the time when Macmillan was Resident Minister in North Africa. In those far-off days Macmillan had imprudently followed Churchill's example, and treated De Gaulle with lofty condescension. It was a mistake. Condescension, as Talleyrand once remarked of treason, is all a matter of timing.

Summitless in Westminster, and excluded from the Common Market, there seemed no reason why Macmillan should not drift quietly along until in the fullness of time the Garter and an earldom rewarded him for the years of non-endeavour on his country's behalf. It was not to be. Eden came to grief because of a fatal itch to do something about Nasser; Macmillan because of an equally fatal propensity to do nothing about Profumo. The Suez Canal, Lady Eden bitterly complained, had flowed through her drawing-room at Number 10; the flood of rumour and innuendo about ministerial improprieties, it would seem, flowed everywhere else in the kingdom except through Number 10. Eden had to go because he tried, inappropriately and belatedly, to behave like a Kipling short story; Macmillan because he confused trollops with Trollope.

After Suez, the Conservatives were bewildered and in disarray; after the Profumo affair, angry and embittered. In the choosing of a new leader, the pushing and shoving to get to the front took place for once on stage instead of, as is the usual procedure, in the wings. It was not an edifying spectacle, and the resultant choice – a disclaiming 14th earl (truly today whoever would keep his earldom must lose it) – was scarcely calculated to restore morale and win an election.

Yet perhaps the Conservatives chose more wisely than they knew in preferring Home to Butler; Bertie Wooster to Jeeves. As in a game of strip-poker, they have shed everything, down to the jockstrap – empire gone, and Kenyatta and Nkrumah necessarily preferred to Dr Verwoerd and Mr Ian Smith; Britannia no longer ruling the waves, or even Holy Loch; admirals without ships, and missiles from over the water; Conservative freedom too circumscribed to be even mentioned. Better, in such circumstances, a 14th earl who thinks he is fully clothed than wily old Rab prancing about in the nude.

The real harm of this 13 years of Conservative government has been that it has offered the country no sort of purpose, not even a misguided one. It has been a time of political, economic and moral free-wheeling, with the encouragement of every sort of soft indulgence, from betting and bingo to the Beatles. Nothing was said or done by those in authority which could possibly seem worthy of remembering hereafter; they all things common did and mean on that unmemorable scene. The records set up have been in road accidents, hire-purchase, juvenile delinquency and telly-viewing. It is the politics of the trough, into which we, the electorate, are invited to bury our snouts for another five years.

Spectator, 6 November 1964   *Alan Watkins*
MR WILSON AND THE COMMONS

Let us begin at the beginning, and go on from there. The fundamental fact about any Administration is that it cannot rule unless it can secure a majority in the House of Commons. This has been interpreted recently as if it were a mere matter of numerical majorities, of head-counting: 'one is enough' is a maxim of Sir Winston Churchill's which has been quoted with approval on the Labour side in the past week. Mr Harold Wilson, of course, has a majority of slightly more than one. Is he therefore free to behave exactly as he chooses?

One cannot help feeling that Mr Wilson and his supporters have confused two separate procedures. First, there is the pushing through of the so-called Socialist measures; of the renationalisation of steel, for instance, and the establishment of the Land Commission. Second, there is the handling of the House of Commons as a corporate body. Mr Harold Macmillan used to be fond of remarking that power in Britain stemmed from the House of Commons, not in the legalistic sense of parliamentary sovereignty, but in the sense that authority in the country depended upon a basis of authority by the Prime Minister in the House. It was an authority which Lord Attlee, and Sir Winston, and Mr Macmillan (except in the latter months) all possessed in their different ways. Sir Anthony Eden did not quite have it; and we all know the consequences of that. Can Mr Wilson establish himself as a parliamentary Prime Minister, and can he do so quickly?

It is perhaps surprising that the question should have to be put at all at this stage. For years and years – at least ever since he became Shadow Chancellor of the Exchequer – it has been assumed that, whatever Mr Wilson's defects, he was a master of the House of Commons. There was no one, it was said, who was quicker at picking up the mood of the House than he; no one who could put a more telling question to a Minister. He was fluent, and witty, and knowledgeable; he had been chairman of the Public Accounts Committee; he seemed to have a genuine feel for the place. Mr Wilson, in short, appeared the complete House of Commons man.

And yet . . . and yet . . . anyone who heard his speech in the debate on the Queen's Speech on Tuesday must have come away with grave doubts as to Mr Wilson's ability to dominate the House of Commons as he should. This was the performance which will go down in political history as the 'leper' speech. In headline terms, maybe, it will not rate so highly as Aneurin Bevan's 'vermin' speech: but its political effects, in the context of the House of Commons, may well be greater. For let us be clear about what Mr Wilson did: as Prime Minister of Great Britain, making his second appearance in that capacity in the House, he singled out for attack a back-bencher who had not yet made his maiden speech. Mr Wilson not only predicted that Mr Peter Griffiths, the Member for Smethwick, would be shunned and avoided; he also implied that it was perfectly right and natural that this should be so. And he did so in words either of extraordinary anger or of extraordinary insensitivity.

One interpretation which was heard after Mr Wilson's speech was that his attack on Mr Griffiths was planned down to the last phrase; that, moreover, Mr Wilson was not in the least surprised at the reaction his assault provoked. Harold, it was being said in the lobbies, is too old a hand not to know what he is doing when he makes this kind of remark. According to this theory, Mr Wilson's object was to demonstrate to the House, and through the House to the country, that he intended to be a tough, uncompromising Prime Minister. And this he succeeded in doing.

One suspects that this version of events puts an exaggerated faith in Mr Wilson's powers of crystal-gazing. Indeed, it is an illustration of a curious tendency to regard Mr Wilson as some kind of super-Calvinistic deity. On this exalted view of him, if such-and-such happens, it must have been because Mr Wilson wanted it to happen. He both sees the future and wills it. But the truth is that on Tuesday Mr Wilson made a major parliamentary blunder. To those who listened to his speech, it was clear that he intended to provoke not the Conservative back-benchers but the Conservative leader. The use of the phrase 'parliamentary leper', though no doubt calculated, was meant as incidental to his challenge that Sir Alec should disown Mr Griffiths. Sir Alec, very wisely as it turned out, refused to be drawn. The storm broke around Mr Wilson, and he did not seem to know quite how to handle it. It was left to Mr Emanuel Shinwell to make a clumsy appeal for the Speaker to protect HM Government. There was no one else; there were no cheers from the Labour benches; to put it crudely, Harold's boys let him down. He had misjudged the mood both of the Opposition and of his own supporters.

And, after the Opposition had subsided, Mr Wilson never really recovered. The House was flat, and so were his phrases: 'false sense of complacency', 'sharper cutting edge', 'dynamic drive'. There was even an attack on the 'Tory press' – fine rousing stuff for a Regional Rally, no doubt, but hardly likely to extract a cheer from even the most dedicated Socialist in the House of Commons. In fact, after the 'leper' incident Mr Wilson did not raise one full-throated cheer from his own side. It was as if the Labour back-benchers sensed that something had gone badly wrong, and that there was nothing they could do about it.

The truth is that Mr Wilson simply cannot afford to have scenes of this kind. The Queen's Speech is one of the longest on record. If Labour is to carry out its programme, it is going to need all the parliamentary time, and all the parliamentary good will, that is available. The whole of social security is to be remodelled. Lord Gardiner is pressing for an early Act to set up his law reform commissioners. There will have to be another Act to create the office of Ombudsman. Above all, steel is to be re-nationalised by (so far as one can gather) setting up a public corporation which will take over the twelve largest steel companies. It is altogether too simple to say that, because Mr Wilson has a majority of five, he can push the programme through. Parliament is the most curious of groups, and unless Mr Wilson can convince it, as an entity, that he is behaving as a Prime Minister, he will find himself in difficulties. It is a matter of style, of technique. Mr Wilson, in other words, has to unlearn a number of the tricks which he picked up in the long years of Opposition.

Let us return to his speech of this Tuesday. Mr Wilson, as he himself admits, acquired his parliamentary wit after years of hard endeavour. Gallons and gallons of midnight oil have been consumed in the enterprise. It is a type of wit which depends, not on a reaction to circumstances as they arise, but on a carefully prepared use of words. The result is that Mr Wilson, though he can be funny, can also be forced. This did not matter when he was Shadow Chancellor, or Leader of the Opposition. But phrases which sound amusing and even penetrating in a Leader of the Opposition can sound quite otherwise when uttered by a Prime Minister. On Tuesday Mr Wilson was still speaking as Leader of the Opposition. There was no message from on high, no vision of the new Jerusalem. Instead Mr Wilson was in there mixing it, as in the carefree days of old; and the technique did not work.

Nor is this only a matter of Mr Wilson convincing the House.If he cannot convince the House, he cannot convince the country. The Commons is still the place where political reputations are made and maintained. It has survived the rise of mass parties, and it will survive television. Somehow, the impression which a politician creates there transmits itself to the country as a whole. Mr Wilson has still to show that he can dominate the House of Commons as Prime Minister. If he cannot, all the statesman-like TV appearances in the world will be no substitute.

New Statesman, 23 July 1965   *Bernard Levin*
AM I A JEW?

Well, now. I have a Jewish name, but there is many a Gentile Isaacs, so why not a Levin? I have a Jewish nose, though oddly enough I cannot see its Jewishness in a mirror, only in a photograph. In any case, it is a meaningless test. The good Dr Morris Fishbein, who in the course of his researches into this subject undoubtedly measured more noses than any man has measured before or since, concluded that there was no such thing as a 'Jewish' nose, or that if there was, it was possessed by so many undoubted Aryans that there was no way of ensuring that the Jews would win – or lose, for that matter – by a nose.

There are more persuasive, though still superficial, arguments. I like Jewish food, Jewish jokes, hold some traditionally Jewish beliefs, such as the respect for learning. (I can remember to this day the shock of incredulity I had at school when a non-Jewish friend told me that he had had a great struggle to be allowed to take up his scholarship. His uneducated father's attitude – more common then than now – had been that 'What was good enough for me is good enough for my son.' This attitude was absolutely inconceivable in a Jewish home.)

None of this will provide any real evidence, though. I was brought up on Jewish food, and the fact that I enjoy it is only an index to the strength of early environmental influence. Jewish jokes appeal to me because of their underlying gallows-humour, which I like because I am at heart a melancholic. I still laugh when my sister tells the story of the *kreplach*, not because the *goyim* can't understand it, but because of its Thurberesque suggestion of the frailty of human happiness and the prevalence of unreason. And the respect for learning is, I should have thought, a universally desirable trait.

Of course, I am begging the question. I know perfectly well that I am a Jew; what I am really inquiring into is what this means to me. Let us start with religion. I rejected Judaism more or less as soon as I was old enough to have any understanding of what religion was about. All religions have their obsessions with form, ritual, observance. I don't know whether I feel further from Judaism than from most religions because its particular observances – the dietary laws, for instance – seem to me sillier today than their equivalent in, say, Roman Catholicism; or whether the savage monotheism of Jehovah (or

Nobodaddy) repels me. I think that there are parts of the Pentateuch that are about as nasty as anything I have ever read anywhere, but you might also say the same thing about St Paul.

Of course, one would have to be very dull of spirit not to find beautiful and fine some aspects of Judaism. A well-ordered *seder* (the Passover-eve family service) is a very remarkable experience – but to me largely aesthetic. I have an uncontrollable revulsion at the sight of someone lighting a cigarette from a candle (some Jews who have long rejected Judaism feel sick at the sight of someone putting a pat of butter on a steak), because I was brought up to look upon a candle as a holy thing. I no longer believe consciously that it is a holy thing, but I do believe that it is a beautiful one, and its use to light a cigarette seems to me vulgar and belittling. Such objective religious sympathies as I have are with the quietist faiths, like Buddhism, on the one hand, and with a straightforward message of salvation like Christianity, on the other. I am unable in fact to accept any of them, but can imagine myself a convert to several faiths; not Judaism, however.

Race, then. Aha. First, I accept what biology and anthropology tell me about race and its attendant oceans of nonsense. There are no innate superiorities or inferiorities; even if there were, there is no such thing as a separate Jewish race, though there may be a race of Semites. (The Jews in modern times have found their greatest antagonists in the Germans and the Arabs; with the former they have many of their most deeply-ingrained characteristics in common, and with the latter their very race.) There's something in this more than natural, if psychology could find it out. Besides, suppose there was a Jewish race, and I was of it; what would follow from that? There is a Negro race; membership of it implies that you are black, but need imply nothing else. So you may be a nice Jew or a nasty one, a clever or a foolish, a generous or a mean, a clubbable or a solitary. I can list my qualities and defects; more meaningfully, I can get a candid friend to do so. I can give myself marks down the list; but for the life of me I cannot see that, whatever the total, it adds up to anything I have in common with Mr Jack Solomons or Mr Ewen Montagu QC.

Which brings me to the only point at which there can any longer be room for doubt. The concept of race is too completely exploded to provide a fair test. Let us think not of race, but of psychology and characteristics. *Have* I anything in common with Mr Solomons or Mr Montagu? If so, what? And if I have not – which is what I believe – have I entirely dissolved any meaning in my own life, indeed any objective meaning at all, for the word Jew?

There is an interesting paragraph on this point by Bernard Berenson, though it seems to me to demonstrate the opposite of what he was arguing.

A Jew is the product of being cooped up in a ghetto for over 1,200 years. His conditioning from within and without, the outer pressure driving more and more to defensive extremes, the inner clutching to rites, to practices, to values making for union and for safety, the struggle for food and survival, the lust for pre-eminence and power: all have ended in producing the Jew, regardless of what racial elements originally constituted him.

Precisely; then the Jew is nothing but a conditioned reflex to a conditioned stimulus (who could have thought the behaviourists could help us here?). And although the idea seems capable of bearing the weight of a considerable structure of generalisation, it falls down as soon as you look at Israel. If a hardy, martial, fair-haired and blue-eyed people are now the heirs of Zion, surely the case for environment is proved? When Herzl's trumpet finally felled the walls of the ghetto, Jewry won her greatest victory. Why, Israel even has her own anti-semitism, in the discrimination of the Ashkenazim against their culturally more backward brethren from the East. Perhaps it will go like this, then. While the Jews of the Diaspora become more completely assimilated – the rate of intermarriage continues to grow, generation by generation – Israel will become more and more remote from any of the traditional concepts of Jewishness. She is still heavily influenced by theocracy; but the ultimately inevitable *Kulturkampf* must break the rabbinical power and turn Israel into a modern secular state.

This may mean that the last test of the *déracinés* will become their attitude to Israel. I think I can clear myself here, even after the severest Positive Vetting. My attitude to Israel – admiration for the incredible achievements, hope that it will continue, combined with the strongest condemnation of her crime against her original Arab population and the campaign of lies she has waged ever since on the subject – does not seem to me to mark me off in any way from a Gentile of similar political outlook. And the other obvious crude test – one's attitude to the Final Solution – I claim to pass with marks above the average, insisting that the slaughter of Russians by Stalin in not much smaller numbers and for no less wicked and senseless reasons should be equally condemned.

And I cannot see that there are any valuable babies that I risk emptying out with the bath-water of my rejection of any concept of Jewishness. I can admire Spinoza or Disraeli or Menuhin just as much without my judgement being affected by any thought of their origins, and I have the additional advantage of being able to despise Ilya Ehrenburg without any reservations.

Has it come to this? Has an idea so old and tenacious, so provocative of generosity and malice, good and evil, responsible for such prodigious outpourings of words and deeds ceased to have any meaning at all? For me, it has. Yet I must face the last logical barrier, the same in effect as the first logical barrier that surrounds Christianity. How can such an idea have survived and conquered half the world, if it is not true? Similarly, how can Jewry have survived, how indeed can she have continued to attract the attention of anti-semitism, if there is no such thing?

Only here am I conscious of any logical weakness in my position. For to an anti-Semite I could not bring myself to deny that I am a Jew, and I would not only not dream of changing my name, but think the less of the Courtenay-Cohens and Lipschitz-Logans for doing so. Yet time will surely take care of this problem, too (plus the fact that the antis have now got somebody else to pick on; not even Dr Fishbein can measure away the Negro's blackness). The world now has no excuse for not knowing what anti-Semitism can lead to, and actually does, on the whole, show signs of amending its attitude accordingly.

And now it is the others who will be increasingly exposed as illogical. If you do not consider yourself Jewish enough to go to Israel, and not Judaistic enough to go to the synagogue, what is left but a vague necessity to belong? And this will disappear, or at any rate be dispersed, with further intermarriage and assimilation; so, of course, will the superficialities attributable to upbringing and environment. The proprietor of my favourite Jewish restaurant tells me that a high, and growing, proportion of his customers are not Jewish. For my part, I reserve the right to go on laughing at the story of the *kreplach* while not particularly caring for the *kreplach* themselves.

Spectator, 30 July 1965   *Unsigned*

THE QUIET REVOLUTION

The Tories' cautious flutter with formalised democracy in choosing their leader has worked with smoothness and despatch. The party, weary of arguing up hill and down dale about leadership problems, wanted a quick decision and got it. It is now plain that the process itself, and the result it produced, represent a revolution within the Tory party. That it was also a polite revolution when it came to the crunch is something that Tory MPs (some of whom will bear the scars of Blackpool for life) can congratulate themselves upon.

There can be no doubt that Mr Heath's takeover indicates that a

radical alteration in the Tory ethos is in the making. If the logic of his
election is followed through, it is possible to foresee a significant change
of attitude among a massive public which has been alienated from old-
style Conservatism. And Mr Heath is not the man to let the impetus
towards change slacken off now. Mr Grimond, in some handsomely
frank words at the weekend, was evidently reckoning with a new appeal
to Liberal voters from a party led by Mr Heath. The same kind of
extension of the Tories' appeal to many who found themselves voting
Labour last year is highly probable. The decisive section of the
electorate which harbours no enthusiam for socialism, but which
shrinks from the strains of the 'Eton Boating Song' and all that
nonsense about grouse moors, is due to come under a new influence.
The party battle-lines will never be the same again.

This can be said not merely because of Mr Heath's kinship with the
unprivileged meritocracy, but also because as a politician he has shown
a readiness for change and an eagerness to innovate which suggest a
fine iconoclastic fervour; and the times offer all too much opportunity
for such a reforming approach to the national problems. It was a jolting
coincidence that linked Mr Heath's arrival at the Tory summit with a
fresh salvo of warning signals about the economy and yet another
shuddering application of the brakes by Mr Callaghan. Even as the
Tory decision was taking shape, the Chancellor was stunning his own
back-benchers with the shock of his third budget in nine months. The
Government is still struggling desperately to restore confidence
overseas, and this week's austerities are an attempt to buy it at the price
of shelving many hopes and promises.

It is early to guess how the country will take this latest Crippsian
sacrifice. But recent history does not suggest that Mr Heath's task will
merely be to hold his party steady and wait until the Government's
failures and misfortunes bring about a return to power. Labour has
already shown itself confused and ham-fisted in tackling pressing
national problems, yet the Tories have so far failed to persuade the
nation that the decision last October went the wrong way.

Sir Alec, unselfishly and rightly, decided that with another leader
they had a better chance of getting their case accepted. Mr Heath may
be expected to put at the centre of their case the need for a radical, non-
socialist, liberating approach to our cobwebbed industrial set-up. The
case will have to be carried with conviction to those numerous
influential, educated, unprivileged members of the salariat who have
looked with a cold eye upon the Tory party hitherto. Mr Heath is well-
equipped to speak to this section of the community. The coming clash
should be exciting and stimulating for Britain. Next week's censure

debate will provide a resounding opening. And the real argument, it must be remembered, is about which party can unlock the shut doors and closed minds of Britain — about whether socialism or a system which trusts to the freedom and enterprise of the individual can get the country out of its mess.

This week has brought evidence of the Tory party's ability to evolve and adapt, once it has been given a helpful shove or two from within. Mr Heath himself is by nature very willing to shove mightily. 'We're a Conservative country,' Mr Maudling once said, 'that votes Labour from time to time.' It was a general truth which may not have a specific application in the convulsions and tensions of the late 1960s. The Tories' new leader can take nothing so comfortable for granted. Perhaps we may offer him a thought which appeared on this page on polling day last year: 'No man can or should lead this country unless he is prepared to bulldoze his way through the road blocks to progress; not for the sake of change, but because change is our ally.'

Spectator, 8 April 1966   *Shirley Williams*
THE CLASS BARRIERS CRUMBLE

Fighting a constituency gives one a worm's-eye view of an election, hardly the best vantage-point. I used to hurry back for the late-night election round-ups to find out what was really going on, but they never seemed to know either. It was an election obscured by a blizzard of facts, polls, forecasts and comment. I'm not sure I can discern its shape yet.

Some impressions, however, remain. Fundamentally, it was a serious, even a solemn election. I don't mean that all the crucial issues were discussed in detail, though I think they were more discussed at the constituency level than some commentators allow. But one had the feeling that the electors had weighed the parties in the balance, made up their minds, and decided, long before the gale of argument was loosed on them. Many attended meetings, more than did in the 1964 campaign. They attended politely and with concern. They wanted to learn, not to be amused. They deprecated the parties' slanging matches. Indeed, if there was one particular weakness in the way the Conservative party fought its campaign, it was its negative tone. Labour might be accused of complacency, but that was much less damaging. The mood of the election was pragmatic, not ideological, and this the Prime Minister clearly saw. Conservative attacks on

Socialism as doctrinaire and inflexible looked irrelevant and out of touch against that massive calm.

Not that the Conservative campaign was a bad one. Mr Heath showed himself to be both incisive and energetic. He talked about real issues. And he firmly dissociated himself from some of the grubbier elements in his party, who were only too willing to find out what mileage the Conservative cause might make by exploiting race and crime. Consequently Mr Heath helped to make the 1966 election a more rational one than 1964. It was much less lively, true; but it came closer to the things we really ought to be debating.

In essence the whole election boiled down to one question – *their* thirteen years or *our* seventeen months. Their thirteen years had reached their zenith in the late 1950s and 1960; the smart young couples buying their first new car, the conventional mock-Tudor semi-detached on a mortgage, the laughing well-dressed children, all stock figures in the advertisements, carried conviction then. So did Vicky's Supermac, the conjurer, the consummate politician, the benevolent but wily builder of 300,000 well-appointed houses. And then it had all collapsed into the usual tedious payments crisis, and into a pay pause, and into an opportunistic sort of *dolce vita*, leaving behind a feeling of mild national indigestion which even Sir Alec Douglas-Home's version of modest living in high places couldn't quite dispel.

So the thirteen years awoke mildly disagreeable memories. This wasn't fair to some of the achievements of those years, but it was a reasonable assessment of their mood – easy, comfortable, evasive. And against that background, the stern warnings of Mr Heath, coupled as they were with a multiplicity of promises and half-exploited issues, failed to carry conviction.

The seventeen months also had their share of events disagreeable to the electors. Perhaps chief among these was a rash of rate and rent increases in the weeks immediately preceding the election, which reminded people of the autumn 1964 little budget, with its higher taxes on petrol, cigarettes and beer. I think these were the factors that led to some abstentions among the least well-off Labour supporters, including some old-age pensioners who in straight economic terms had improved their position. Another element that created some disaffection among traditional Labour supporters was the incomes policy. It is, in my experience, widely misunderstood. Many people believed that the proposed early-warning legislation outlawed all unofficial strikes for ever, or that it ruled out any pressure by a trade union for higher wages. Once it is spelt out in detail, much of the suspicion disappears.

But the curious thing about this election was that those groups who benefited little, if at all, in economic terms from the Labour government swung most strongly in its favour. Better pensions and the abolition of prescription charges are not of the first moment to young men and women in their late twenties and early thirties. Housing is, and Labour's inability to fulfil the pledge on housing mortgages within the seventeen months might have been expected to be very damaging. Furthermore, the swing to Labour was especially high among junior professional and executive occupations, men and women often hit fairly hard by high taxes and concerned with incentives. Yet nearly everywhere, the Labour vote from the new private housing estates dramatically improved.

The reason was again simple. For electors under forty, the post-war Labour government was part of history, not autobiography. Children at the time, they had associated it with shortages, austerity and a grey middle-aged society. In the thirteen subsequent years, the picture of the Conservative party as the natural, the almost inevitable governing party had been well and truly established after three successful election campaigns. So it came as a surprise to discover that the Labour party could govern too – and govern effectively. Man for man, the seventeen short months showed that Labour ministers were at least as good as their Conservative counterparts, and often more hard-working. The seventeen months laid to rest the persistent myth that the Conservative party alone understood how to govern Britain. And the laying of this myth justified the Prime Minister's conduct of the last Government, for he acted throughout as if his majority was a fully adequate one.

The class structure of British society still plays a significant part in its politics. Where that structure remains largely intact, as in the most rural constituencies, the swing to Labour was small. The deferential vote counted. But in the urban, and particularly the fast-growing constituencies, its importance is decreasing. The traditional loyalties, too, are disappearing. Another decade or so may spell the end of class politics in Britain, among younger voters at least.

Harold Wilson and Edward Heath have both played their part in this realignment. Wilson's great achievement has been his capacity to project himself as a national leader, attracting support well beyond Labour's normal loyalists. Heath has not yet had time to project himself beyond the traditional Conservative supporters, and to some of them was perhaps less appealing than his predecessors. But once the tradition of a ruling class dies, and it is now nearly dead, the Conservatives are wise to move to a leader who represents class mobility and not class stagnation. Macmillan in a sense did too, but his image was one of Edwardian unconcern. He merged imperceptibly into the world of country houses and grouse moors. Heath has not done so, wisely; but it is still difficult for people to identify themselves with him. His appeal ought to be to the younger technologists, scientists and teachers, like Harold Wilson's, but his life is manifestly unlike theirs. Hampstead Garden Suburb, a family and golf are more everyday and comprehensible than Albany and the organ.

For the Labour government, the next two years are crucial. They will be decisive for the economy and for the pound. If Labour can balance the books without large-scale unemployment, with a fair rate of growth, it should become the usual governing party. But that is to ask for a great deal. If it allows unemployment to rise and stay fairly high – 3 per cent or more – it will fail even if the deficit is removed, because unemployment will force the unions back into defensive poses – a thought that might be considered by those economists who advocate a permanently much higher level of unemployment. If it maintains the demand for labour, but runs into further balance of payments difficulties, it will come under tremendous pressure from our creditors abroad. Harold Wilson recently described 1966 as 'make or break year' for Britain; it is make or break year for Labour as well.

New Statesman, 9 September 1966   *K. S. Karol*
MAO'S SECOND REVOLUTION

The present explosion of 'popular anger' in China recalls the first year of the Russian Revolution rather than China's own revolution of 1949, the year when power passed without disorder – particularly in the towns – into the hands of Mao Tse-tung's victorious army. The Chinese communists boast that in 1949 their discipline prevented violence and excesses. Today they have handed over the towns to 'angry masses' led by the Red Guards and, while advocating caution, they declare in a Central Committee resolution: 'Chairman Mao has always taught us that a revolution cannot be accomplished with much elegance and delicacy or with much kindness, friendliness, courtesy, moderation and magnanimity. The masses must educate themselves in this great revolutionary movement and learn to make the distinction between what is just and what isn't, between the ways of acting correctly and incorrectly.'

What does this communist revolution mean in a country where the Communist Party has been in power for 17 years? How is it possible for the leaders of a country to rejoice at the sight of young rebels shutting down shops which have been long nationalised, invading offices of the administration and even looting museums the state has established at great cost? If the Chinese government had simply wanted to purge the administration and to change the education system and the cultural policy, it had the means of doing so by decree without unleashing this mass movement, which inevitably involves excess and which disrupts – if only temporarily – the life of the country. What is to be gained, therefore, from this strange revolution and what are the ends it seeks to achieve?

When the first demonstrations against the leadership of the local party took place in Peking, most Western commentators talked mainly of the struggle for the succession to Mao: events have not supported this theory. Mao is more active than he has been for years and seems to be in no hurry to leave the political scene. The Party hierarchy has not been notably altered and no top leader has been attacked by name or singled out as a target for the Red Guards. There is no evidence that the present events are the effect of a fratricidal struggle at the summit of the Party.

However, the lower levels of the Party have been seriously shaken and a member of the Central Committee in charge of the cultural sector has been dismissed and violently attacked as a 'revisionist and implacable enemy of the thought of Chairman Mao'. This leader who wanted to 're-establish capitalism in China' is Chou Yang and it happens that I had a very long interview with him during my four months in China. I was with him for five hours at the International Club – at present closed by the Red Guards because it is too 'bourgeois' – where he outlined to me his conception of proletarian culture, which resembled in every particular the ideas advanced by the promoters of the present 'cultural revolution'. Chou Yang seemed to me to be completely 'anti-revisionist' and anti-Soviet: his remarks on Shakespeare ('who never lived the socialist experience and is therefore not very interesting for youth') or on China's classical cultural heritage would never be out of place in a Red Guards' journal. Perhaps he wanted to carry out his programme – which according to him would give birth to a 'proletarian culture 100 times superior to bourgeois culture' – by means of gradual action from above. Today his superiors have decided, on the contrary, that the masses must take affairs into their own hands 'to move more quickly towards the goal'.

Thinking about Chou Yang, I begin to understand a little better the Chinese version of present events. Reading the Peking newspapers, one gets the impression that a great number of 'revisionists' infiltrated themselves into the Party machine to protect the 'bourgeois' intellectuals and 'to follow the capitalist path'. It is against these groups, one might think, that the people and particularly the youth are revolting, and by eliminating them they would be destroying the old society, the 'old customs' and bourgeois ideology.

In fact, from what I saw of China, the reality appears to be altogether different. The Chinese were not previously 'soft' with 'bourgeois' intellectuals and for years anti-revisionist propaganda has been one of the elements of the Maoist programme. But the Maoists do not judge the orthodoxy of Party members by their professions of faith, no matter how sincere. What counts above all in their eyes is the conduct of one's daily life. A good communist is someone who lives in complete austerity and who on all occasions shoulders the heaviest burden. Every official, every intellectual who takes advantage of his position to make his life easier immediately unveils his 'revisionist nature'. It is not by chance, therefore, that the first leaders affected by the purge were those of the Peking Party committee: they inevitably had a higher standard of living, met foreigners and occasionally visited the luxurious International Club with them, as well as the good restaurants and the 'de luxe' shops whose existence is so violently attacked by the Red Guards. It is possible that one of the 'great crimes' of Chou Yang might be just this.

It is true that Chou Yang was neither a czar nor a Kerensky and Mao could have dismissed him without resorting to a 'cultural revolution' of such magnitude. But perhaps he considered that a discreet purge would have no educative value for youth and the population as a whole. And it seems to me that his aim is precisely to inculcate the revolutionary spirit into the new generation by battles and mass movements, which may appear to us Westerners entirely fabricated and perhaps even harmful, but which are certainly exciting and without doubt taken seriously by the Red Guards.

In the West one can hardly believe that such movements, patently inspired from above in order to attain limited objectives (which could perhaps be achieved in other ways), could be greeted with genuine enthusiasm. This whole 'cultural revolution' therefore appears to be purely artificial. But when one knows the very special political climate of China in recent years one can understand that once the impassioned – not to say fanatical – young generation are set in motion (even by order) they are difficult to control. It seems to me also that the provincial and municipal leaders have not always been aware of the intentions of those who inspired the cultural revolution and that, when faced by Red Guard demonstrations, they may have reacted as 'guardians of order' instead of taking over the leadership of the movement. Obviously this error of judgement has been fatal in that it 'unveiled their revisionist character and their fear of the masses'.

Another point is that until recently the Maoists' internal policy has not been free of contradictions. On the one hand they preached a quasi-evangelical egalitarianism and, rejecting material incentives, relied solely on 'ideological incentives' to develop their economy. On the other hand they were, in a certain sense, 'gradualists' in that they partly maintained the privileges of 'national capitalists', to whom they paid considerable incomes after nationalising their factories, and preserved an education system (particularly in the universities) in which until recently 50 per cent of the students were of non-proletarian origin.

By launching the 'great cultural revolution' Mao Tse-tung and his associates have therefore tried to kill two birds with one stone: to give the young people, for the first time, an opportunity to act, and at the same time to take advantage of their action by eliminating certain situations which were becoming inconvenient to the system. But it is probable that the young militants, eager to act, may have seized on the occasion to form themselves into Red Guards and that today they believe themselves to be the heirs of the Russian revolutionaries of 1917 and the Chinese revolutionaries of 1949.

The Chinese leaders are no doubt delighted at this zeal shown by the new generation and its devotion to the Maoist cause. For some time the Maoists had wondered how to protect their successors from the virus of apolitical and bourgeois attitudes which, according to them, is responsible for the 'decadent evolution' of the Soviet Union: apparently they now have proof that China's youth is immunised. It has been demonstrated that the revolutionary spirit is not dead in China, and that she will not lack volunteers to push back the Americans if they cross the 17th parallel in Vietnam or attack China.

This means of defence compels Mao to renounce certain others which apparently could have been as useful to him. Indeed his 'great cultural revolution' lays the foundation stone of a real Maoist 'church', but it also perpetuates what may be a definitive schism with the USSR and with the world communist movement. For Mao, 'Sovietism' and 'revisionism' are synonymous and express a perversion of spirit unworthy of true communists. The 'revisionist' is an egoist, an unstable character in whom one can have no confidence, he explained to the Red Guards who are charged with purging the Chinese administration of the elements suspected of these vices. Having decreed that the Russians are the embodiment of evil, having allowed those who resemble them to be persecuted in China as the worst enemies of the revolution, Mao can no longer consider any joint action with the Soviet Union except at the risk of completely disconcerting and demoralising his own supporters.

What is paradoxical in the present situation in China is that, in order to consolidate and re-launch the revolution as they intend, they have adopted a hard line which inhibits any reliability in their relations with the communist bloc and at the same time runs the risk of restricting the spread of the Chinese revolution in the world. For if it is true that great mass movements are the best school for revolutionaries, those taking place in China at present are composed of a very special type of activist who is quasi-religious and more conditioned by the fact that China is an essentially rural country than by the old tradition of the Western workers' movement.

What is now happening in China is isolating her more and more from the rest of the world. All the developments are so particularly 'Chinese' that one cannot find any equivalent either in any other country or in other communist parties. Some wish to see in the present cultural revolution a simple manifestation of neo-Stalinism because China, with some reason, feels herself encircled, as Russia once did, because the cult of Mao is as intense as that of Stalin once was, and because it displays great contempt for culture and freedom of thought. One also remembers that by a strange coincidence the Russian purges were carried out in a particularly violent manner 17 years after the revolution.

It is a fallacious comparison. In the Soviet Union the purges were a police affair, conducted with all the power of the NKVD. Mao works in an entirely different way. It is the Red Guards who, at his summons, track down the 'revisionists' in order to 'educate them by persuasion' and not to deport them. In short Maoism is a completely different thing from Stalinism and much more genuinely revolutionary.

An editorial in *Granma*, central newspaper of the Cuban Communist Party, recently invited the 'Chinese comrades, if they were in the mood, to listen to the advice that they should stop making themselves ridiculous.' Personally I don't think that the Maoists are in the least ridiculous. Their revolution is taking a direction that disturbs us and which risks compromising their relations with the other movements of the Left – particularly in Europe. There is certainly no cause for rejoicing on our part: developments in China will impoverish us all. But this ought not to lead us into vain and facile condemnation: this will merely have the effect of aggravating China's isolation and of prolonging the excesses taking place there. It would be much better to try to understand the very special and tragic conditions which have brought about this distortion of the Chinese revolution: China, over and above Vietnam, remains the main target of American aggression, and by virtue of this fact alone, she is the vanguard of the resistance to the *Pax Americana*.

Spectator, 22 April 1966 *Ludovic Kennedy*
LIBERTY'S MUDDY FOUNTAIN

Like some hidden but slowly festering sore, of whose existence we have all been aware for some time, the evidence in the Moors case finally broke last Tuesday. 'David Smith will say that he stood in the kitchen and was reading the label on one of the bottles when he heard a scream – a very loud, long and shrill scream. He then heard Hindley shout from the living-room, "Dave – help him." Smith ran into the living-room and stopped just inside the door. He saw Evans lying half-on and half-off the couch. Brady was standing astride Evans, hitting him with this axe round the head and shoulders.' Later, in an alleged statement by Brady: 'After that the only noise from Eddie was a gurgling. David and I cleared up the spot and the gurgling stopped and we cleaned up the body.' Back to the Attorney-General. 'Then Brady said to Hindley, "That's it. It's the messiest yet." He asked Hindley if she thought anyone had heard the screams of the youth, and she replied: "Yes, my grandmother. I told her I dropped a tape-recorder on my toe." ' And finally: 'The body was tied up, Brady said, and Smith helped Brady carry the bundle upstairs. Later Brady said, "Eddie is a dead weight," and the two accused started laughing.'

Some or all of these allegations, and others, have been published fully in all the national newspapers. Descriptions of the first day's proceedings were given a double-page spread in the *Sketch*, *Mirror* and *Express*, a whole-page spread in the *Sun* ('Woman lured brother-in-law to watch axe murder'), *Telegraph* ('Children's Secret Fate'), and *Mail* ('Left Luggage led to Graves'), and a half-page spread in *The Times*. We know, as a matter of fact and not opinion, that more, much more, is to come; and we know, too, that during the five weeks that the trial is expected to last, the national press will give it the same ample coverage.

This means that there will not be a literate man, woman or child (and what child, after the age of ten, is not literate these days?) who will not be given full access to all the details of what is undoubtedly the most macabre murder story in modern times. Now it is important to state here that all one is discussing is allegations and evidence. In law the two accused are innocent people. Nothing has been proved against them, and it may be that nothing will. We do not know this, and we will not know it until the jury reach their verdict. But that is not the point. The point is whether it is desirable that such allegations and such evidence, much of it beyond what any of us could imagine in fantasy or nightmare, should be made freely available to the public at large. What will be the effect of reading such evidence on young (and old) innocent minds? Will the knowledge that such things are possible tend to deaden even further our sensibilities in regard to permitted violence? Will it, contrariwise, disturb some people so profoundly as to have a permanent or even temporary effect on their health? Worse, will already unbalanced minds entertain the possibilities of emulation?

At first consideration there would seem to be an excellent case for affording the public some sort of protection. A benevolent censorship is, after all, exercised in most other forms of communication. A film which showed what is alleged to have occurred in the Moors case would be lucky to get an 'X' certificate, if it got one at all; a play dealing with the same matters would certainly not be granted a licence by the Lord Chamberlain. No reputable publisher would print a novel containing what is alleged, and even the disreputable ones rarely go as far as this. But censorship of any such hypothetical film, book, or play, is more likely to be exercised at source. Because the Moors case is concerned – above all else – with what is alleged to have been done to children, it is improbable that any such book, film or play would ever come to be written. Are there then not good grounds for a judge to rule in his discretion that the press may only report such evidence in any case as he allows, or even to forbid them to publish any evidence at all?

In theory yes. In practice no. The real difficulty is in laying down a general rule. Judges, like the rest of us, differ in their own sensibilities and in how they feel the sensibilities of others. While some might feel that the public should be protected from the details of the Moors case, others might find, say, Christie's necrophiliac activities far more shocking. Where is anybody to draw the line? With such a rule some judge, sooner or later, and with the best intentions in the world, would be hearing all his cases behind closed doors. Press and public would become deeply and rightly suspicious of what was going on. Justice would no longer be seen to be done.

But what is even more important is the right of all of us to know what is going on around us, whatever it may be. Say, for the sake of argument, that what is alleged to have happened in the Moors case is in fact the beginning of a new and terrible anti-social trend to be followed by other, similar cases. If we were to be protected from any knowledge of this, we would be in a most dangerous and impotent position. One needs to know the full details of the situation, and this may include the full horrors of it, in order to take action on it. Parents need the knowledge of it to keep a closer watch on their children. Social workers need the knowledge of it to investigate its causes. The police need knowledge of it to prevent it recurring. This knowledge may distress us deeply, some more than others, but it is the price that any society must ultimately pay for its own good. Knowledge, as Daniel Webster once said, is the fountain of all liberty; and he drew no distinction between knowledge good and bad.

Spectator, 19 August 1966   *David Rees*

THE VIEW FROM ROT-HILL

> Here while the town in damps and darkness lies,
> They breathe in sunshine and see azure skies;
> Each walk with ropes of various dyes bespread,
> Seems from afar a moving tulip-bed,
> Where rich brocades and glossy damasks glow
> And Chintz, the rival of the showery bow.

Ever since Thomas Tickell, Addison's editor, wrote this near-doggerel in 1722, Kensington has remained well apart from central London. The chintz and the showery bow in Kensington Gardens have been replaced by stretch nylon and the disturbing transistor, but from Kensal Green Cemetery to the Fulham Road, and even to the river with the amalgamation of Kensington and Chelsea last year, the area remains tenaciously residential – even if the contrasts of squalor and opulence inside the royal borough are probably greater than in any other administrative area in the British Isles.

The historical background is less complex than many London boroughs. There is a Domesday reference in 1086 (Mr William Gaunt, in his study of Kensington, bravely speculates that 'A tribesman called Cnotta may have been the Saxon Napoleon of Notting Hill'), followed by a medieval church and manor ('Abbot's Kensington') developed over the parallel lines of the two Roman roads to the south-west, preserved today in High Street and Bayswater Road. Then, in the seventeenth century, came the three great houses, two of which remain to this day. First, there was Holland House, blitzed beyond repair in the second war and now a youth hostel; it was followed by Campden House, which stood near today's Sheffield Terrace, where the Notting Hill plateau begins its descent to High Street; and lastly, came the Palace, rebuilt from a slightly earlier house by William III, whose statue still stands in front of that austere façade as he stares at the traffic on Kensington Road.

At much the same time the 'old court suburb' of Kensington Square sprang up, and King Billy's successors built the Orangery and laid out Kensington Gardens, together with the Round Pond and the Broad Walk. During the next century the hamlets of Brompton, Earls Court and of the 'gravel pits' around the toll-gate of Notting Hill congealed until the great building boom of the nineteenth century produced the Kensington of today – in appearance the most Victorian of all London boroughs; it seems only fitting that the title of royal borough was given in the year of the Queen's death. Thus the literary and historical associations of the borough lie heavy on the ground, impossible to escape: the Palace and the Georgians; the Square where Thackeray and John Stuart Mill lived and worked, and ruined now by the shadow of the big stores; Holland House with its roll call of the great from Horace Walpole to Macaulay; and the later Victorian circle of G. F. Watts and his adherents in 'Little Holland House' in the area of the present-day Melbury Road. One can see why Eliot, who was a churchwarden at St Stephen's, Gloucester Road, at first thought of calling his great poem 'The Kensington Quartets.'

But the artistic, high-bourgeois world of the Victorians and the Edwardians has long since vanished; perhaps it lingered on until 1939, merging on the way into the image of Kensington as a place of stifling respectability, now an inaccurate image which yet still endures.

Yet out of this old Kensington that ended with the war has emerged a new Kensington centred around Notting Hill Gate. Like the old Kensington, its boundaries are imprecise. It extends southwards from Westbourne Grove, sprawling into Bayswater and Campden Hill towards Kensington High Street. From east to west it runs along the line of Bayswater Road–Holland Park Avenue, from Arnold's 'lone, open glades' of the Round Pond to the gardens of Holland House. From north to south its great axis is the line of Church Street and the Portobello Road, that fantastic, half-mile-long world's fair that plays every Saturday.

In the shadow of the 200-foot-high slab of Campden Hill Towers which rose at the rate of a storey a week out of the wreckage of the old Gate in that affluent summer of 1959, lies the new, reconstructed Notting Hill Gate. Moreover, in the last few years Notting Hill has been on the tourist track as never before. When the blossom comes out during late April in Brunswick Gardens, people make movies about it, and quite rightly. Yet there are still echoes of other forces of the universe in the high crime rate; the small hours are disturbed by bawling fights and the tearing, rending sound of insolent chariots as they drive into each other and leave shattered glass on the pavements for the morning.

Yet these are excrescences; in the pubs on Church Street and the Portobello and in the afternoon drinking clubs there is a serious, relentless search for distraction. And here, perhaps, one may invoke two great writers, Ezra Pound and Wyndham Lewis, whose spirit lies over Notting Hill. As Miss Patricia Hutchins has recently reminded us in her study of *Ezra Pound's Kensington*, it was in 10 Church Walk, off Holland Street, that Pound found his 'Kensington Graveyard' in the years before 1914. It was Pound who called the area Rotting Hill, and so well did he know Kensington that when he came to write the Cantos a lifetime after his days in Church Walk we can see that he remembered in great detail that lost Edwardian Kensington. Moreover, long after he met Pound in pre-1914 Kensington, Wyndham Lewis settled down in the 1930s at 29 Notting Hill Gate, a site now demolished to make room for the re-development scheme. But Lewis returned to Notting Hill after his disastrous war-time exile in North America, and there he wrote both *Rotting Hill* and *Self Condemned*, continuing to live at No. 29 until his death in 1957. (The friendship between the two men endured to the end of Lewis's life; less than three years before his death we find Pound writing in December 1954 'to confirm HIGH opinion of "Self-Cndd"/it and Rot-Hill all, past 2nd hell lit/yet discovered among ruins of Albion. Shd/git yu the Nobble . . .')

Yet reading of Pound's days in Kensington one realises how little the area has changed. The physical structure of the district is unchanged, in spite of all the surface rebuilding and the acres of progressively decaying houses now turned into rachitic flats and bed-sitters, those streets in North Ken where entire lorry-loads of rubbish are dumped under cover of darkness – a 'growing menace,' according to a recent issue of the *Kensington Post*. What is new, replacing the effortless sense of superiority and progress that buttressed that earlier royal borough, is the sense of *uncertainty*: for, manifestly, in the Notting Hill Gate of the mid-1960s the centre has long since ceased to hold. Down the road to the Gate, past the trees and seedy Victorian elegance of Pembridge Square, is the sign-board of the 'Sindh Sufi Philosophical and Mystic Society; teachings and publications of the Sufi sages of the East.' In the local newspaper shops the *Occult Gazette* (next month: 'The Auric flame as the Birth of divinity') sells by the quire, a splendid example of the quintessential fifth-century atmosphere of Rot-Hill, a memorable synthesis of sophistication and barbarism.

So today, the Genetesque storm-troopers, the rich kinksters on the

Portobello and the switched-on birds in the boozers perform the Rotting Hill follies; tomorrow, who knows? One can only hope that this Cockaigne of debauched Patrick Hamiltonian respectability, etiolated, drunken Saturday afternoons and lazy days close to the reassuring Orangery with its bust of Marcus Aurelius will at least last for a little longer before it finds its Gildas . . .

> and the Serpentine will look just the same
> and the gulls be as neat on the Pond,
> and the sunken garden unchanged,
> and God knows what else is left of our London,
>   my London, your London.

(Canto 80)

Spectator, 10 March 1967   *Simon Raven*

A LETTER TO MY SON

MY DEAR BOY,

Very shortly now I must congratulate you on your fifteenth birthday. Fifteen will be a difficult age for you, I think, as it is the age at which you will be refused, for the first time, the indulgence due to a child while also being refused, as yet, the privileges of a man; and it will be more difficult than ever these days, since so many fifteen-year-olds are now being allowed to ape the airs and pleasures of their elders, which can only make you, who will *not* be granted this licence, confused and jealous.

However, you should understand that in most cases this 'teenage' liberty is merely a brief prelude to lives of inexorable drudgery . . . to the early marriage which proletarian habit dictates, the tenancy of a jerry-built breeding box on a council estate, and the routine performance, for forty years and more, of some wretched manual or clerical task, which will be all the more tedious for the so-called 'technological' methods of our era. It is precisely in order that you should escape such a fate when you are adult that we shall deny you, in adolescence, the trivial freedoms which you may covet in others; for while they are out in the streets and bowling alleys, courting each other (and their own future servitude) over bottles of Coca-Cola, you will be at the carefully chosen school where you will acquire (I hope) the poise of mind and body necessary to one who would pass an adventurous and pleasurable life.

At the same time, it has occurred to me that you may, at your age, think three years more of (relative) confinement a stiff price to pay for a good which is only in prospect; and it is certainly true that schoolmasters, as I remember them, do not do as much as they might to mitigate the rigours of present restriction by a proper explanation of future benefits. Still less do they explain (for these excellent men often have little of the world in them) the elementary principles which ensure the full enjoyment of such benefits. As your father, I am taking it upon me to discharge this office; for you are old enough to understand what I shall say, and you have several years in hand during which you may rehearse, before you come to apply, the rules of life and conduct which now follow.

But first, a word or two about the theory behind these rules. 'The world,' as a celebrated philosopher remarks, 'is all that is the case.' Human conduct, therefore, can only depend on our knowledge of human affairs within the world, and that knowledge only on what we have observed to be true beyond reasonable doubt. Now, the only thing which *is* true beyond reasonable doubt of humanity in this world is that, as another celebrated philosopher remarks, 'man is born, man suffers, and man dies.' You should not be unduly put out by the word 'suffer', which in this context only means 'has things happen to him'; even so, the maxim is not encouraging. But such as it is, *it is all that we can know*; anything else is either speculation or cant.

And again: if the world is all there is, and if all we can be sure of is that we will spend a limited time in it, then clearly we had best spend that time seeing and enjoying as much of the world as we can in circumstances as pleasant as possible. It is to this end that you are receiving your careful education; and to this end that I lay down the rules of life and conduct to which I now revert.

The first of these, the cornerstone of the entire code, is to ensure your independence, your freedom to come and go as you please. Since the chief threat to this is posed by those who want power (the natural enemy of independence) you must place yourself beyond their reach. You can do this (even now) if you possess money; but such money you will first have to amass, as I have little to give you, and those who want power will make it increasingly hard for you to do so.

It follows, then, that you should find a continuous means of livelihood which is yet compatible with freedom of movement. My own is one such, but there are few others that are not actively criminal. The best I can do is to suggest that you keep your eye open for those occupations (however precarious) which entail the minimum of supervision with the maximum of travel; and for the rest I must beg you to try for the best academic qualifications you can, as these may help you to the more exciting and 'privileged' kind of work . . . the only kind you want. Of course, it may turn out as time goes on that the only way to achieve independence of others will be to acquire power yourself; but this possibility has implications which I do not care to consider.

While we are touching on money, remember that it is not your business to pay anyone else's way any more than it is his business to pay yours. So if you *must* lend money, consider the loan as lost; and if you must get into debt, do it with spirit.

Now, if money is one means to independence, a noteworthy obstacle to it is premature marriage or any serious form of sexual entanglement. So let us be very clear about two things:

(1) Eschew marriage until you can well afford it in *addition* to everything else you want. And let us in no case at all have any of that whining, such as we hear from so many pestilential young couples, about its being society's 'duty' to subsidise your folly. If you want to set your wife up in a house, then find one first and buy it. Don't put on that pathetic young lover's look and expect someone else to wave a magic wand.

(2) Sex outside marriage is an agreeable (if sometimes overrated) entertainment. If somebody fancies you and you return the compliment, then away to the hay-loft and the best of luck. I would go still further: do not, while you are still young and wholesome, neglect any tolerable opportunity which offers in this line (even if you don't feel particularly keen at the moment), or you may live to regret it too late. If I'd known *then* what I know now, I'd have been far less fastidious than I was (not very). This said, however, do take care lest your erotic interests preclude others more important, for this condition is as big a curse as marriage.

Always be kind and considerate; but always make it plain, before you start, just what you are offering – which should not be a lifetime of devotion but merely a few hours' diversion. If you feel yourself becoming infatuated, and therefore liable to say more than you really mean and get yourself into trouble, follow Lucretius his bidding: make a deliberate and detailed inspection of the paramour's less appetising features, and sanity will soon be restored.

A last word on this subject. Don't get a bastard and don't get poxed, either issue being damnably awkward and both easily avoidable if you make a few simple purchases before you open your breeches. The chemist, remember, comes cheaper than the surgeon.

If you are in full control of yourself both financially and sexually, then you are your own man and pretty well set. However, we should not omit the more important minor matters.

Drink. Don't drink too much before meals, or you won't enjoy them. If you must make a hog of yourself, do it during or after dinner, by which time you will at least have something solid to be sick on.

Gambling. Don't gamble with friends, as it is painful to win from them; but if you have something to spare, by all means risk it in a reputable casino against an anonymous bank or strangers. (Take cash, never your cheque book.) Do your football pools regularly: the outlay is nugatory and you may win a quarter of a million.

Religion. Church of England (if you really must). This is a quiet and decent superstition, as they go, offering a wide choice in decoration and no poisonous enthusiasms.

Politics. It is impossible, as things now run, to side sincerely with either party. Time was when a statesman's province was to secure the country against its enemies without and to maintain good order within. This was all any rational man required of him. Nowadays, however, politicians whether of left or right (there are no longer any statesmen on either wing) occupy themselves ever more spitefully and deceitfully in escheating the property of those who have the energy and wit to get it in order to feed yet higher the envy of the rest.

The Conservatives are more moderate and certainly less rancorous in their demands than the Socialists; but at bottom both parties are doing much the same thing – fleecing the able to conciliate the feeble. This they do in the name of 'human equality' or 'social justice,' thus seeking to flatter with meaningless phrases (for no two men were ever yet agreed on their meaning) the stupidity and sloth of those whose votes they require in order to exercise their passion for interference . . . at your expense and mine. This brings us back to the whole question of power versus independence. Politicians now demand to lead our very lives for us, and the only way of stopping them is to keep as far out of their way as possible and constantly on the move.

And so we come full circle. Enough for this birthday, I think . . . except for one more piece of advice, à propos of nothing at all, but in keeping, perhaps, with the spirit of such festivals. *Never part in anger*. However much someone you know has annoyed or even injured you, if he is going a long way away you must have him to your table and drink his health: as I shall yours, my dear boy, on this your fifteenth birthday, for which pray accept the fondest good wishes of

YOUR FATHER

New Statesman, 18 August 1967   *Gerda L. Cohen*
JERUSALEM REVISITED

It feels like a city afflicted by schizophrenia, flung into drastic and hazardous recovery. Politically, you would define it otherwise: a capital regained by Israel, or a rudely-ingested chunk of Hussein's kingdom. According to your viewpoint. But political statements, though true, cannot convey the truth of here and extraordinary Now. Therefore the images of delusion recur, insistent. For 19 years, each side of cleft Jerusalem has seen the other side as a closed institution for the dangerous unknown, happily kept behind barbed wire, evoking the most fearful curiosity. Imagine the inmates, suddenly let out by some crackpot administrator. Amid the rubble, they meet and gawp. Over the bramble wire, people interrogate each other's features. Their appalling similarity can no longer be concealed. Christian Arab or Moslem Israeli or North African Jew? You cannot tell them apart. 'They're so horribly like us,' admitted a Hebrew teacher queueing for the Number Five. 'At first they stood in line, but now they push harder than born Israelis. If it weren't for their tweed jackets – really, I couldn't tell . . .' Up came the bus, wedged solid, and a grim, perspiring phalanx fought to get on. Victory over the Arab Legion has doubled the population of Jerusalem, without doubling the transport system. Impregnable, the socialist bus barons don't give a damn. Since their cooperatives hold a monopoly, not even the wretched Minister of Transport can prevent them from running tours to Bethlehem while the citizenry fume. 'Our only hope,' said a Talmudic gentleman from the town hall, 'is the Arab bus driver. Independent (thank the Ineffable Name) and steadfast in their refusal to join the cooperatives. Our holy city will yet have a decent service (if it please the Most High) provided the Arab drivers are not bribed into socialism.'

Who will ever forget crazy Thursday? That mauve, arid morning when the frontiers vanished; blown away by the dry winds of Judea. Officially, united Jerusalem began at noon. But nobody took any notice. 'I've waited 19 years,' said a housewife in a ritual wig, 'so why should I wait another two hours?' The policemen understood. Before the sun whirled high, Damascus Gate was a-boil with jeeps, truant officials, infantry somehow on leave. At first the Arabs were afraid to venture into Jewish Jerusalem. They sauntered through Jaffa Gate,

clung together at the bump of exploding mines, went chaperoned by
relatives from 'occupied Palestine'. But within a week they had
captured the city: their city, now. Gangs of *shabab* in tight pants roam
the Supermarket, palping meat none can afford, accosting every female
with a loud 'Shalom!' until the manager, driven beyond political
consideration, groans in helpless rage. Too late to recriminate. The Old
City kids, unleashed from their alleys, have conquered the sole park in
central Jerusalem. They gallop the roundabouts; somersault down the
unbelievable greensward; make pi-pi in the municipal oleander – and
stay on till dusk, for ex-Jordan Jerusalem had neither park nor
playground. 'The obvious solution,' declared a steely member of the
League of Labour Women, 'is to open kindergartens for them,' and she
rattled a tin with righteous ferocity.

While the politicos bumble on about 'free access to the Holy Places'
everyone has found out the real problem: access without asphyxiation.
The Holy Sepulchre offers a horrid example. On a Sunday, broach it at
your peril. One by one, multitudes squeeze down a marble burrow to
emerge at the altar over His grave. Hung with entrancing baubles,
ablaze like a Christmas bazaar, foetid with old breath and frankincense,
it cannot be endured for longer than a moment. Protestants are repelled,
Jewish visitors baffled, and the rest struck radiant, kindling each a
candle in hypnotic silence. Women elbow viciously to touch the insipid
Madonna pent up in gold. You squeeze out again, ducking to avoid the
alabaster bunions.
Three dominant rites – Latin, Orthodox and Armenian – share the
Byzantine church built around this cave and the wondrously gilt upper
floor called Calvary. Millennia of squabbling have at least given each
rite its niche and appointed hour. Even the Coptic and Assyrian
priesthood fling up their dark antiphony at agreed intervals. Since 1956,
the church has been under repair. Why so long? Inquiry will evoke an
ambivalent shrug. 'We go slow in case it fall down,' offered a Greek
Orthodox acolyte, his epicene beauty ogling the gloom.
Before the Six Day War, Christian Arabs in Israel were allowed into
Jordan once a year: generally at Christmas, seldom at Easter. This
pilgrimage meant foremost a family reunion, because the Arab family
remains a clan. Thrown asunder by war and migration, the clan
persisted. Now the shrines of Jerusalem celebrate a triumphant kinship.
Outside the Holy Sepulchre, families from Nazareth and Jericho seem
to fuse in a perfumed, weeping arabesque. 'We are all together,'
explained a Nazareth uncle. He adds: 'Except for my sister in Beirut
and my aunt in Amman, very unfortunate poor lady . . .' A hush fell,

while the nieces gazed at their modest organdy pleating. 'We do not know what will become of aunt,' said the uncle from Jericho.

Most Israeli Arabs are Moslem: debarred, until the war, from a shrine approaching Mecca in sanctity. It lies in a great square of silence, the city thrusting close about. Even when thousands congregate, space and grandeur dwindle them to ants. Made perfect by the flagstones' vast simplicity, the Dome of the Rock shines out, a huge golden egg set upon emerald tesselation. 'Not gold,' said the *kadi* in charge, 'anodised aluminium gift from Egypt.' 'Please take off shoe on entry,' he rapped, his eyes blank, at the loud tourists from Tel Aviv. Commando boots and peasant sandals clutter the bronze gateway. Under the Dome, caged by intricate splendour and a billion rich minutiae, is a naked rock. No more dramatic monument could be conceived. 'From this rock, Mahomet leapt to heaven!' The *kadi* used the same prosaic monotone as before. The aluminium cupola and the Prophet's ascension on his favourite horse are both beautiful facts. And why disbelieve? On Friday, armed sentries keep out everyone except the faithful, who arrive in charabancs from Galilee and Gaza and the West Bank. Nobody, unless provably Moslem, can even approach the great square. From a turret window you may watch the host of Islam gather. At noon a howl of ecstasy arose from the minaret: a terrible wail of devotion like the cantoral wail in synagogue. It rose and fell, thwacked by exploding mines.

'Yesterday they were knifing each other and today – just look at them.' A Polish dowager shook her dyed frizz at the Israeli soldiers in Cafe Nasr-e-din, hob-nobbing with Arab youth over the jars of pickled radish. 'I feel whiter and whiter every day,' she said bitterly. But the Moroccan Israelis felt at home. Sub-machine guns slung on the coat-rack, they devour genuine kebab – not the neutered pap which passes for it in Tel Aviv. So too the Old City market. Fobbed off with a European imitation – a hygienic pretence – they'd forgotten the genuine article. No wonder Israelis rush into the labyrinthine market like mice down a cobra. You cannot budge for crushed flesh in Khan el Zeit. Wagons collide head-on, squirmy with offal. Above the heaving tumult you catch the strangled entreaty of porters, bent double under a fresh-slain sheep whose bubbly white fat knocks black hats off an excursion of bewildered churchmen. A Franciscan attempts to extricate his skirt from a cartful of goat. For them, nothing has altered except the exchange rate. 'The Jewish government not play so fair,' complained a merchant amiably. 'We lost about three bob on every pound sterling.'

'But you lost the war, didn't you?' retorts a German customer, also amiable. They chuckle in accord, eyes opaque with mistrust. On Via Dolorosa, trade seems to lag. Olive-wood carvers go on turning out tableaux of the Nativity. 'Can I buy some wooden animals *without* Jesus?' asked a lady from Hendon. 'I'm an agnostic, you see,' she told the impassive proprietor. By the end of the day he was left with a forlorn group of Jesuses. Life in near-feudal Jordan had been dirt cheap, giving the peasantry enough to eat and the *mukhtar* enough to squander. Israel, inconveniently, enjoys high wages and a higher cost of living. In Jerusalem, the two economies collide. Arab tradesmen protested against the taxation consequent upon this economic clash by shutting up shop for one day last week. They can afford to go on strike, having trebled their prices, whereas public employees earn what has now become a pittance.

Beige dust continually blows about the Old City – from the razing of emplacements which hid Arab Legion snipers and from the bulldozing of little stone hovels to clear ground for a new Jewish quarter. The old quarter, beseiged in 1948, was blown up later by the Arab Legion, or casually desecrated. Arab families, unspeaking, pile their household on to a waiting Army truck. Rabbis trot about, their kaftans floury with dust, trying to identify a long-defiled Bible seminary, whose tenants had just been sent to a village near Hebron. There does not seem any end to the dismal cycle of dispossession. The Israel government has promised to compensate Arabs who once lived in New Jerusalem. But some want more. A lean and dark-suited gentleman loped into the neat Jewish suburb of Beit Hakerem, gave his patent-leather toe-caps a polish and rang a door bell. 'It's my house,' he told them, in faltering Hebrew remembered from 1948. 'Can I come in, please?'

Spectator, 17 November 1967   *Denis Brogan*

DOWN WITH NORTH BRITAIN

I returned a few days ago from a visit to my native land during which Scotland was suddenly very newsworthy, especially to the inhabitants. There was, for example, the disaster at Montevideo in which the chairman of Celtic rebuked his own players, while most of the people I talked to were in favour of dropping Mr George Brown on Buenos Aires by parachute.

But the real event was the Hamilton election. It would be going too far to say, as the French duke said to Louis XVI, 'Nay, sire, it is a revolution'; but Mrs Ewing's triumph, so widely welcomed – even by supporters of the defeated candidates – shows up the astonishing constipation of the two 'dominant' parties. Mrs Ewing, I am told, was an extremely attractive and effective candidate. The Unionist candidate was a young man who may be all right when he is older. The Labour candidate, whose name I have already forgotten,* was a miners' official who was given the nomination as a piece of trade union patronage in what was assumed to be a trade union rotten borough. There seems to be a conscious breaking away from the general domination of Scottish life by genuine Englishmen and bogus Scotchmen.

It will be said (it has been said) that many of the Scottish grievances are sentimental. They are. But sentimental grievances, as we should have learned in this modern world, are extremely powerful. The Conservative party, or the Unionist party, or the Tory party as run from London, is psychologically unsuited to deal with these sentimental grievances.

The Scottish aristocracy and the Scottish upper middle class have for a long time revealed their Scottish patriotism by wearing often bogus tartans at Highland Games, usually as bogus as the tartans; the middle class by shouting 'feet' at international rugger matches at Murrayfield. In Ireland, people of this type were known as West Britons: these were and are North Britons.

The leadership of the Conservative party consists not only of noblemen of really ancient pedigree (there are far more noblemen of really ancient pedigree in Scotland than there are in England: *pace* Miss Nancy Mitford); but there are also a great many people who did well out of armaments in the First World War and out of whisky in the Second World War. Above all, none of them gives a plausible impression of even conceiving the possibility of preferring the interests of Scotland to the interests of Britain.

It was a Scottish poet who wrote the best poem about London, but he did not accept London as his capital as, in practice, so many eminent Scots have done. (As a resident of Cambridge, I realise I am myself open to a *tu quoque*, which I accept as just.) This feeling of being betrayed by their natural, or unnatural, leaders has grown in Scotland as the brief period of economic expansion came to an end, except possibly for Edinburgh, in 1919. When the second greatest Glasgow poet, Robert W. Service, came back to his native city after fifty years in the Klondyke and elsewhere, he said that no city he knew had changed less in that time. This represented stagnation. A great architectural journal last year wanted Glasgow preserved as the most

* It was Wilson, as it happens – Editor, *Spectator*.

magnificent Victorian city in Britain. But a great many people in
Glasgow don't want it preserved as a Victorian city, physically or
spiritually.

On the economic arguments for more Scottish control of Scottish
business, there is a great deal more to be said than is normally said by
the tradition-bound bankers and economists of Scotland. It is true that
more money is spent per head on social services in Scotland than is
spent in England. But a great deal of Scottish money is spent in support
of extravagances (as Mr Ludovic Kennedy has pointed out) which may
appeal to Mr Julian Amery in Brighton but have no great appeal to the
people of Skye, Dumfries, or even Edinburgh.

The British Empire was supported by the Scots as long as it paid
them. That gloomy pipe tune, 'The Barren Rocks of Aden,' sounded
tolerable when Aden was a necessary way station to India, which was
candidly described in my school geography book before the First
World War as 'the brightest jewel in the Crown,' followed by a
complacent statement of how well the Scots did out of this jewel.
Sentimental passion for empire was never very strong. There is none
now. There is also no empire, a point more clearly seen from Glasgow
than from Brighton.

The Scottish Nationalist movement has its lunatic fringe. I met last
week a zealous Nationalist who insisted that not only must the English
yoke be thrown off, but Edinburgh and all of the Lothians and
Berwickshire must be pushed into England because they were 'Anglo-
Saxon.' There are good arguments for having far more control of
Scottish affairs really exercised in Edinburgh. Nonsense about being
really governed in a Scottish way from Saint Andrew's House in
Edinburgh is even less plausible than the pre-1922 argument for
Ireland's being governed from Dublin Castle. There are many things in
Scotland which the English would do well to imitate if they could. For
instance, the very superior legal system. But the point is that many
things have been forced on the Scots which *may* be good for them, but
are forced on them with a remarkable lack of tact. Mr Ted Heath, for
example, dismissed the Scottish Nationalists as 'flower people':
presumably he knows better now. Earlier he had expressed delight in
being in Glasgow, a centre of 'soccer.' This game is unknown in
Scotland. The game of football, usually called 'fitba,' *is* played.

Scotland is not prepared to be broken up into Ulsters, as is suggested
by the Honourable Quintin Hogg. Nor is the explanation given me by a
Labour man, that the Orangemen were ordered to vote for the Scottish
Nationalist, to dish the Labour party, very plausible. In fact, the time
has arrived for a really great debate as to what the future of Scotland

should be. I have no enthusiasm for the appearance of Scotland between Saudi Arabia and Senegal at the United Nations. I have no great enthusiasm for establishing a customs barrier between Scotland and South Britain. But I have a great deal of enthusiasm for encouraging the renewal of courage and hope.

The English have a great deal to learn, but on the other hand, as I frequently tell the Scotch, the Irish, and the Welsh, the English are much cleverer than they are – once they decide what is the clever thing to do. I make two suggestions: that the Honourable Quintin Hogg be told to shut up; and that Mr Edward Heath get some competent expert on this strange country which he visits, it seems to me, with no more real comprehension than Mr Podsnap. As for the Scottish Labour party, it is remarkably sterile of leaders who might really think of the legacy of Keir Hardie instead of being content to be Mr Wilson's poodle.

But the best comment on Hamilton and the best comment on the disarray of the Scottish establishment is provided in the gossip column of a rival paper to the SPECTATOR, a column edited by somebody using the initials PHS. The minister of Saint Columba's, Pont Street, welcomes Mrs Ewing's victory very tepidly and thinks the Scotch should settle for influence at Westminster. This is a confusion of influence and power which I am surprised to find in a Scot and a Presbyterian. Some of the others are simple or nauseating or both. One London Scot kindly tells us that Scotland is not viable since all the able Scots have left the country. Another who seems to belong to the school of Scots (and their English friends) who think the country begins at Perth, announces that it is a musical comedy affair. Another takes up the hollow old Edinburgh joke that the Scots really run England anyway. This was not true even when the 'heids o' departments' were all assumed to be Scots. All most of these bureaucrats did was to 'respectfully homologate' the orders of their English superiors.

I have been wondering who these Scottish rulers of England *are*. The only first-class politician who is a member for any Scottish constituency is Sir Alec Douglas-Home. Mr Jo Grimond might be if he had a more secure political base. I have been reflecting on the people who have made the news in politics and finance and business in the last ten days or so. There are Messrs Wilson, Brown, Callaghan, Crossman, Macleod (who sits for an English constituency), Foot, Jenkins, O'Brien. There is Mr Weinstock; there was Sir Paul Chambers. Sir Isaac Wolfson, who has just given a great gift to Cambridge, is a Glasgow man by birth and education who is far more generous to England and Israel than to his native country. I may have missed one or two Scots, but they cannot have been very prominent. I have also missed 'the choir invisible' of Scottish Nobel prizemen.

Scottish conceit was irritating enough when it had some justification. It is maddening now, and the people of Scotland are aware of this. Douglas Hyde, in one of his early tracts for the Gaelic League, saw its object as the saving of 'our Ancient Irish Nation' from 'sinking into a West Britain.' For a great many Scots of the type consulted by PHS, being North Britons is superior to being a Scotchman or a Scotsman. Indeed, to be a North Briton living in South Britain is the real culmination of their felicity.

About a century ago, Walter Bagehot said that Adam Smith's view of human history was that it consisted of the progress of man from the state of barbarism to the state of being a Scotchman. Smith exaggerated a little bit. But what he or Mr Hume would have thought of these drab figures in London I refuse to state. It is known that Dr Smith could use bad language on occasion.

Spectator, 24 November 1967   *Unsigned*
MR WILSON SAVES HIMSELF

The *Spectator* unreservedly welcomes the Government's decision to devalue the pound. For the best part of two years we have consistently advocated this course – at first alone, more recently in the company of a growing number of other commentators and experts, but always as part of a reviled minority. We have urged devaluation, not because we regarded it as desirable in itself, but because it was essential to the health and strength of the British economy. We have consistently prophesied the failure of the Government's previous policies to provide any solution to the country's chronic balance of payments problem, let alone any prospect of a reasonable rate of improvement in living standards at home; and so it has proved. And we have urged the drastic step the Government has now taken, after three years of denial and repudiation, not as a panacea, but as the *sine qua non* of any cure at all.

Not that the decision was taken as a result of our or anyone else's advocacy. It was taken as a result of the inexorable pressure of events. When, a few weeks ago, the Chancellor of the Exchequer informed the Prime Minister that the prospect was for an even larger balance of payments deficit next year, just as this year's is bigger than last year's, Mr Wilson suddenly found himself in the position of Mr Ramsay

MacDonald in August 1931, faced with the choice between saving the pound, by a policy of savage deflation that would shatter the Labour party, or saving himself. MacDonald chose the pound, and in the event saved neither. Mr Wilson, perhaps benefiting from this cautionary precedent, chose to save himself.

Why he failed to devalue long before it became a simple matter of self-preservation to do so – for, let there be no mistake, it is Mr Wilson and Mr Wilson alone who is responsible for the criminally negligent delay in taking this inescapable step – is something not susceptible of rational explanation. But whatever the cause of the Prime Minister's purblind obstinacy, it has forced the nation to endure three utterly and unforgivably wasted years; three years in which every other objective of policy has been subordinated to the maintenance of the sterling exchange rate, and in which every sacrifice made to this end has been in vain.

But this is not a time for looking back. The important question now is whether the devaluation can be made to work – made to transfer sufficient resources from the home market to exports to create a quick and healthy balance of payments surplus. Already, two of the principal props of the anti-devaluationists' argument have been demolished: few other countries, and none of Britain's main trading competitors, have cancelled out our advantage by devaluing in turn; while – in spite of the present excitement in the gold market – there has been no world monetary chaos. For these initial successes the credit belongs to the international financial community and to the Treasury officials at home who implemented the Government's decision.

Unhappily, other omens are less favourable. By delaying devaluation until he was forced to take this step, Mr Wilson has done it in a way that creates the least possible confidence in the act and in the new parity. Nor is this the only consequence of delay. It has meant borrowing more money abroad to buy more time at home, and hence a greatly increased cost of repayment. It has meant that an act whose success depends on the exertions of businessmen and workers has been postponed until, thanks to the Government's previous measures, the goodwill of both sides of industry is all but exhausted. And it has meant that the putative export boom is now timed to coincide not, as should have been the case, with recession at home, but with a strong recovery in the domestic economy as well. Unless the inflationary dangers inherent in this situation are firmly checked, the devaluation cannot possibly hope to have more than a temporary success.

It was principally to curb the incipient boom at home that the Chancellor announced, in addition to the new rate for the pound, the various other elements in the devaluation package. They do not inspire great confidence. The abolition of the export rebate and of the selective employment premium, together with the increase in Corporation tax (a particularly destructive example of the Labour Party's anti-profits reflex), will have little effect on consumer demand at home: their chief result is to reduce the true value of the devaluation to some 11 per cent (before allowing for any increased costs from the devaluation itself). Economics is not an exact science. We needed simply the biggest devaluation that our competitors were prepared to tolerate without following. This proved to be around 15 per cent. But to whittle that down still further, unilaterally, *before* it has had time to take effect (for obviously the export rebate would have had to go ultimately) is madness.

As for the other measures, the hire-purchase controls are limited entirely to motor-cars, and the promised cuts in the rapidly rising total of public expenditure are derisory. Of course, the devaluation itself – through rising prices – has a deflationary impact on spending at home. But it is only too clear that all this is far from enough, and to make the devaluation 'stick' and avoid a blaze of inflation the Government is gambling heavily on the success of its incomes policy – an incomes policy, moreover, which, after the events of 1966, the Government dare not make other than voluntary. This would have been a poor straw to clutch at a time of constant prices, rising unemployment, a government with authority in the country and a trade union movement in control of its members. But to make the success of the voluntary incomes policy the keystone of the success of a devaluation at a time of rising prices (due to the devaluation itself), falling unemployment (which will be the pattern throughout 1968), a government that has lost all moral authority and a trade union movement that is losing control of its members, is to invite disaster.

Yet to allow a devaluation to fail is unthinkable. There is simply no other weapon left. The effect on the country's morale would be incalculable. That is why those who genuinely want a devaluation to succeed always insist on a margin of safety; on erring on the side of initially devaluing too much and deflating too much. There can always be a let-up later, when the operation is proved to have been successful. The present Government has allowed no margin whatever: it has whittled down the amount of the devaluation and not deflated enough. It seems clear that Mr Callaghan, who genuinely wanted to make a success of the devaluation, intended to secure that vital margin, and to buttress the so-called incomes policy, by deflating more. But once again the Prime Minister overruled the Chancellor – just as he overruled and outmanoeuvred him when Mr Callaghan, again rightly, advocated devaluation in July 1966.

This does not mean that the new policy will not work at all. Devaluation is a very powerful export incentive indeed, and to some extent – and for a period – it is bound to work. The question is whether, by other measures – which should include, immediately, further cuts in government expenditure to make adequate room for the hoped-for export boom, and the shelving of the Industrial Expansion Bill *sine die* in order to restore confidence among those on whom the Government depends to get the increased export orders – the devaluation will be allowed to restore lasting equilibrium to Britain's balance of payments, or whether it will be used by the Government simply as a means of winning the next election, its benefits dissipated in a wildly inflationary pre-election boom.

That is the choice before the Government today. And if it is to be left to Mr Wilson, it can be taken for granted that it will be the short-term, ephemeral, objective that is chosen. (No doubt he will convince himself that the long-term will take care of itself: he always does; and that is why the country is in its present mess.) The signs are already there. The inadequate cutback in home demand, so that no margin of safety exists. The withdrawal of Mr Marsh's courageous fuel policy White Paper, presumably to keep open more uneconomic pits – when the right course after a devaluation would have been to keep down the price of energy for industry by abolishing the tax on fuel oil. And the Prime Minister's declaration to the parliamentary Labour party on Tuesday that the economy would grow over the next twelve months by anything up to 6 per cent; a perfectly feasible rate (for one year only) but one that would generate such inflationary pressures that the devaluation would be doomed from the start.

All these signs point in the same direction. And even if there is no failure of will on Mr Wilson's part, there remains the even greater danger of a failure of nerve. Strong nerves will be needed this winter, as unemployment – and prices – rise, as Labour continues to fare disastrously in opinion polls and by-elections, and before the export boom begins to manifest itself, if the Government is to resist the increasing clamour from its own supporters for more expansion and more public spending. The Prime Minister has cheek, but that is not the same as nerve.

It looks increasingly as if all will depend on the next Chancellor of the Exchequer. Mr Callaghan will shortly resign the office he has held for more than three years. It is right that he should do so. He has discovered too late the pit his leader has dug for him; while any hopes he may have of leading a Coalition government without Mr Wilson are, to say the least, premature. Although his culpability for the fiasco of Labour's economic policy during that time is infinitely less than that of the Prime Minister, it is still sufficient to warrant resignation. Nor is this the only case for a new Chancellor. The events of last weekend have gravely diminished Mr Callaghan's personal authority over his Cabinet colleagues. And if a sane economic policy is to be pursued – above all, if some check is to be imposed on public spending – that authority is essential.

Mr Callaghan's successor will be, potentially, in a strong position. He will not have the disaster of the last three lost years like an albatross round his neck. He will be able to enjoy the benefits of his predecessor's devaluation. Above all, Mr Wilson, having just lost one Chancellor, will not dare lose another in a hurry. If, in spite of this, Mr Callaghan's successor allows himself to be the Prime Minister's creature, the chances of last weekend's devaluation proving the beginning of the British 'economic miracle' which it so easily could have been will be very slender indeed. But a new, strong Chancellor – a Chancellor who, as his first move, would introduce a significantly deflationary budget in 1968 (for this, in the light of the inadequate measures taken so far, is vital) – could still do the trick. The nation will pray that he does.

New Statesman, 5 January 1968   *Philip Toynbee*

DICTATORS, DEMAGOGUES OR PRIGS?

Malcolm Muggeridge is obviously right when he claims that the views and values of us Lefties are far from being popular ones. (Though I doubt whether his own opinions are any more widely shared, or whether he thinks the worse of them for that.) This is not a new situation, of course, but recent events have hammered it home even into such comparatively optimistic heads as my own. There *have* been rare moments when the emotional reaction of the majority has coincided with that of the radical minority: at the very beginning of the Suez affair most people were genuinely shocked and indignant at the bombing; and it was only after a few days that wog-bashing resumed its old appeal. But the elections of 1964 and 1966 were not events of this order. On the whole the public voted for the Labour party because they believed that Wilson and Co. were *more competent* than their opponents; more likely to 'solve' our economic problems; to make capitalism 'work'. Heaven knows there was no mandate for socialism, in any single one of its many meanings; not much of a mandate for abolishing capital punishment or tolerating homosexuality or introducing comprehensive education. There was no mandate whatever for making our black minority the *real* equals of the white majority.

Let's admit that even in terms of their electoral image this government has done badly. If their principal aim, from the very beginning, had been to get rid of all our ex-imperial pretensions, all the weapons and bases which serve no purpose except vainglory; if they had started to dismantle the whole antique, ridiculous and expensive apparatus as soon as they first came to power, then we wouldn't be in our present economic mess. What's more, this could easily have become a popular policy at home, where people do at least prefer buying new TV sets to bashing old wogs. It is a policy which would not, presumably, have offended the gnomes of Zurich, etc. since its successful implementation would have increased the strength of our capitalist economy. And if that economy had been strengthened in this way more might even have been done for the poor, the sick, the under-educated and so on. On these terms a radical policy was possible at a minimal cost in popularity.

The usual answer to this argument is the same as the answer given when we protest against the government's wretched support for the American crime in Vietnam. We are economically dependent on the US. If we incensed the American government either by withdrawing from our East-of-Suez commitments or by condemning the Vietnam war, then the Americans would make it unbearably hot for us economically. Obviously there is truth in this answer, and certainly the left-wing extremist counter-argument is utterly unconvincing. We are told that if we adopted 'socialist' policies then we could safely disregard the Americans, the gnomes and our own ever-greedy and grasping tycoons, nationalise those 'commanding heights' which remain, follow a Little England policy and 'withdraw' from our present position as a country which makes its wealth by trading.

This could be done, of course, but only at the cost of a real and drastic impoverishment of the whole nation. Announcing three successive five-year plans, our government would have to announce at the same time a moratorium – shall we put it? – on elections for the same period. The call would be to blood, sweat, tears and no votes in order to create an earthly paradise some time in the future. And we all know by this time how such an appeal would be met: so our native OGPU would soon be in full vigour.

The point I'm trying to make is that the term 'democratic socialist' has become meaningless in our time. Probably it was always meaningless, but the experience of 1964–8 has made its futility horribly plain. Not only does this country not want socialism: it wants to sell arms to South Africa; to remove sanctions on Rhodesia; to do almost anything which will preserve or improve its own standard of living. And if one is a democrat before one is a socialist – as I am; as nearly all 'democratic socialists' are – then how should one react to a situation in which one's most cherished political and social aims are not only unpopular but will certainly remain so in the foreseeable future?

The silliest and most contemptible conclusion is the false-democratic one that we should change our views and bring them into better accord with those of the majority. But it would be almost equally silly to go on thinking in terms of a 'socialist Britain': to go on talking about 'socialist policies' as a possible choice for the present government. The difficult present task for the radical minority is simply to stick to our ultimate aim – the creation of real and universal human brotherhood; to propagate our ideas and to abandon all hope of a realisable socialist society – using this concept simply as a compass to guide us through these harsh seas of present reality. And – most difficult task of all – we have to avoid becoming unbearably self-righteous while we do these things.

There never was any magic virtue in the proles – though I would argue, however puritanically, that to be moderately poor in an unjust society is nothing like so bad for us as to be stinkingly rich. (My own preference is for being moderately rich.) The comparatively poor of Britain want to be comparatively richer; and they want this more than they want anything else which politics can give them. Malcolm Muggeridge deplores this base materialism; but he is in the lucky position of being a prophet, not a politician. He can fulminate because he does not have to operate. And if you must operate – if you are Roy Jenkins, for example, trying to decide, at this moment, what is to be done next – then this general desire for personal gain at the expense of either wider benevolence or saner priorities (better education before better television sets) – if you are a responsible politician of this sort then this is part of the brute material with which you have to work. You have to do good by stealth if you are to do any good at all.

My own conclusion is that while the world remains more or less as it is no Labour government will be able to make *any* fundamental change in the economic structure of the country. Abandon even the most lingering regrets for further nationalisation, which has little to do with socialism at the best of times (how many railwaymen have ever felt that Beeching *et al.* are, somehow or other, their elected work-mates, as opposed to the remote tycoons of pre-nationalisation days?). Concentrate on carrying through as many humanising changes as can be effected in time, remembering that the 'time' will almost certainly prove to be a maximum period of five years. For even reform is likely to prove unpopular, if it is real and thorough. The electorate is unlikely to return a government which has been genuinely concerned with the old, the sick, the under-educated and the very poor rather than with creating a bonanza at home in which the rich get richer and the rest get a little less poor in the process. The electorate is even less likely to return a government which has a strictly honourable record in international affairs: honour can be very expensive these days.

But though a 'socialist' policy is so far outside the hypothetical 'mandate' as to be impossible, a decent radicalism of this kind is unpopular but feasible and legitimate, provided the government acts from the start on the assumption that it will lose the next election if it does its duty as it should. And on this assumption there was no need to kowtow to the Americans in Vietnam or anywhere. A government can endure an adversity which it has deliberately courted on deliberate principle much better than it can bear the (present) adversity which has come upon it by sheer folly, short-sightedness and unsuccessful obsequiousness.

A leftish government may, with good luck, sneak into power in Britain about once every 20 years. Make the most of those five years, not by continuing to confuse ourselves with talk of 'socialist' policies, but by pushing through all those temporarily unpopular reforms which the previous Tory administrations have avoided. Try, above all, to alter the climate of opinion in this country, which should be easier to do in power than in opposition. Abandon all immediate hope of murdering the Capitalist Beast, but try to humanise him to such an extent that he himself will become aware of his own hideousness, and undergo, at last, a voluntary course of plastic surgery.

What it amounts to, in more offensive terms, is simply this: every democratically-elected government cheats the electorate, and the only saint of modern democracy, Abraham Lincoln, not only knew this but constantly put it into practice. The worst form of cheating is to abolish democracy (dictatorship); the next worse is to do what the voters want you to do no matter what the cost in honour, humanity and the future (demagogy), and the least bad is to do what you think right and wise even at the cost of losing the next elections (priggery). I am on the side of the prigs, though few governments are obliged, of course, to make such an absolute choice as I've suggested. A very successful government may manage to be both priggish and popular. I fear that the Wilson administration has been demagogic in intention but wildly unpopular in achievement.

New Statesman, 29 March 1968   *Francis Hope*

DO WE NEED A FOREIGN POLICY?

Or, to be more brutal still, do we need a Foreign Secretary and his attendant office? Mr Michael Stewart is a living embodiment of the socialist schoolmaster everywhere, and we should all be worse off if the species perished. But his re-appointment is not exactly the mark of high necessity. Mr George Brown suffered the unenviable fate of having two horses shot from under him – expansionism at the DEA* and Europeanism at the FO – but at least they were living horses when he mounted them. Mr Stewart has now been called in, for the second time, to ride the corpse. If the DEA is shoved into the Treasury, could the Foreign Office not be integrated with the Board of Trade? This would be in keeping with our new, slimmed-down, export-minded, 'Scandinavian' orientation, and the incumbent President is quite able enough to conduct the business on his weekly half-day.

I have to be joking. Wasn't Mr Stewart's stand over arms to South Africa just the moral commitment Labour voters expect on foreign affairs? And isn't his position on Vietnam, contrariwise, just the sort of wrong but positive gesture which students of Ernie Bevin have learnt to expect from Labour in office? Or, as CND often argued, we could still have a unique moral influence if only we could get our moral priorities right. Or, as the anti-fascist front argued in the Thirties, foreign policy will catch up with us if we don't forestall it with a decent foreign policy. No country is an island, not even us.

The principal answers to this are that foreign policy is expensive and unrewarding; and that it involves one in frequent dealings with foreigners, who are not to be trusted. Take the case of France, where foreign policy has been at the top of the government's list since 1958. By their obsessive concern with external affairs (we are told) the French have beggared their own economy, inflated their own worst communal instincts and made enemies of all decent people. Furthermore, the argument runs, they have not been successful even in their own stupid terms. The General's ostentatious tours in Eastern Europe ('foreign policy') have had less effect than our own much greater expansion of Eastern European trade ('common sense'); French military

* Department of Economic Affairs (now defunct) – K.A.

independence, with all those costly azimuths, is merely a grandiose Swiss nonsense compared with the possibilities of a serious integrated European deterrent; and M. Rueff's irresponsible guerrilla warfare on behalf of gold looks foolish beside the rapid penetration by American capital of the 'up-stream' sections of French manufacturing.

It is true that an overwhelming interest in foreign affairs is the mark of the romantic rather than the rationalist. In one interval of his campaign for the Presidency the patrician John Kennedy asked his speech-writer Theodore Sorensen what cabinet posts he would, in the abstract, fancy. Sorensen's reply was full of Middle-Western progressive sense: 'Justice, Labour, and Health-Education-Welfare.' 'I wouldn't have any interest in any of those,' Kennedy replied, 'only Secretary of State or Defence.' Kennedy-lovers and Kennedy-haters can draw their own conclusions. Students of De Gaulle face a similar Great Divide. Either foreign policy is the determining issue, the big central juicy area of contention and cerebration, or it is a trivially glamorous function of honest administration and rising GNP.

The snag is that the distinction between rationalism and romanticism does not cover all the ground. While Kennedy is still, as it were, on the stand it may be worth recalling an argument often put forward by sophisticates in LBJ's early days: that precisely because Johnson was unromantic, unglamorous and unambitious he would run a much safer and maturer, if less exciting foreign policy than Kennedy had done. Events have not exactly borne this diagnosis out. If Kennedy wouldn't obviously have done better, he could hardly have done worse. Johnson's famous complaint about the difficulty of dealing with foreigners – 'they aren't like folk you were reared with' – is a classic illustration of the mentality which would rather not have a foreign policy at all. Unfortunately, they are like folk you have to live with.

Nowhere in the world does this apply more than in Britain. The Fabian mind is isolationist rather than international, but English history makes it extraordinarily difficult to carry out isolationism effectively. As Lord Attlee said in explanation of his hostility to the Common Market: 'If I must have foreign friends I prefer them to be black or brown.' 'If I must' is the key to Labour foreign policy: George Brown was a startling, perhaps even an honourable exception. Under his influence, we have moved in the opposite direction: instead of trying to have no foreign policy at all, we have tried to have all available foreign policies simultaneously: Atlanticism, Europeanism, the special relationship, East of Suez, the Commonwealth and (over South Africa) hard-headed commercial realism. We can now at least expect some choice between these glittering pluralities.

It is likely, however, to be choice by default. We wound up our
military presence East of Suez not, as we now claim, because we had
definitely opted for Europe (which would not *necessarily* involve such a
withdrawal in any case) but to save money. In the same way we have
chosen to support the Americans in Vietnam not because we believe
they are right but because we need them; we have 'chosen Europe' not
because it has been proved that it will succeed but because our own
economic growth has temporarily failed (let alone because we have
genuinely 'become Europeans' of the Monnet stripe); and we have
chosen sanctions against Rhodesia not because they will work but
because nothing else is morally endurable to the Prime Minister. We are
object not subject, improvisers rather than planners. Things are in the
saddle, and ride Downing Street.

In order to have a foreign policy worth the name, one must have a
view of the world, and views of the world are dangerous, un-British,
counter-empirical things. Gaullism, for example, has a definite
theoretical starting-point: that the old nation-state has by no means had
the stuffing knocked out of it by the 20th century's disastrous wars and
that it will continue to be the basic unit of serious political transactions
for the foreseeable future. Indeed, by Gaullist lights it is likely to grow
stronger rather than weaker in the next decades, as the artificial
predominance of the two super-powers over their clients diminishes.
One may take this proposition as a sad truth or (as the General does) as
an historical glory, but from it certain attitudes follow. Transplants of
Gaullism breed ironies: the first is that non-French Gaullisms would
thrive on opposition to De Gaulle. 'German Gaullism', for example,
may begin by presenting the bill for all the concessions the Germans
have made to the French since 1958: the same old promises of help with
the *Ostpolitik* might no longer be accepted. American Gaullism might
not stop short of declaring war on the French . . .

'British Gaullism' would be a very strange bird, and would probably
include the Anglo-Russian alliance among its plumes. (Membership of
the EEC would be a low priority.) It should go down well in the
constituencies and on the Celtic fringe (though Scottish and Welsh
Gaullism would present problems, like Brittany or Quebec). But it
would demand an intellectual approach to the problems of diplomacy –
or, if you like, a lot of airy-fairy twaddle – which is unlikely under the
present management. Mr Denis Healey, for all his passionate espousal
of the American alliance, would be susceptible to the charms of
intellectual analysis – not necessarily this one. Mr Stewart is less of a
threat to the present system, whereby basic decisions are taken by the
Prime Minister, and the Foreign Office carries out local operations

where clearly identifiable interests are threatened. Gibraltar, Hong Kong, Mauritius – particularly now that the Commonwealth is *de jure* as well as *de facto* foreign territory – are the limits of a Foreign Secretary's domain. Our activities there no more constitute a foreign policy than an afternoon's shopping adds up to a macro-economic theory.

Has anyone something better to suggest? We might, for a start, take Nato's status as an alliance of free nations as seriously as the Danes and Norwegians do, and use next year's renegotiations as a lever on the present regime in Greece: it is not only an undesirable partner, but an unreliable ally. We might take seriously the idea that the General not only means what he says but means what his successor will say: we are an island on the edge of Europe, drastically different in culture, history and interests from the Six. We might reflect, not on isolationism, but on the fact of our present isolation: Mr Wilson's hard work (while the rest of us hoggishly sleep or oafishly shout slogans) rests on a belief that he has a special claim on Russian and American ears. To judge the belief, examine the results.

We might find eventually that we neither could nor should have a foreign policy. Does Italy, does Japan? At least we should know where we stood. Is it a fear of knowing that makes us so reluctant to look, and so keen to disguise our lack of imagination as solid good sense? At the moment we are neither Atlantic flesh nor European fowl nor good little-England red herring. We may not know it, but the world does. Confusion, rather than compromise, has brought us here. Thought alone will not get us out, but thought is where action starts. Is Mr Stewart thinking?

New Statesman, 7 June 1968   *Mervyn Jones*
THAT WEEK IN PARIS

For me it began on the Monday afternoon, 27 May, when I drove my car on to an almost empty boat at Dover. British officialdom saw me off with a mere glance at my passport and 'Sure you've got enough petrol?' Driving up from Boulogne was like driving in Russia – long empty roads, a feeling that I'd just invented the automobile, the only risk a temptation to take the bumps too fast. In Paris the students had mustered 50,000 demonstrators despite a boycott appeal by the Communist Party and scare stories by the police, who claimed to have unearthed caches of arms. My car radio was alarming; another battle seemed quite possible. Cautiously I garaged the car on the Right Bank and started walking.

It was a city of fear, a re-enactment of Paris under the occupation. Shops protected by grilles, cafés and restaurants closed or with a lonely couple of diners, the boulevards deserted as I've never seen them at such an hour (9 p.m.), a few pedestrians walking fast and talking in low voices. An army of police — 50 vehicles, their radios crackling — encamped on the big car park beside the strike-bound Louvre.

I crossed the river and plunged into the Latin Quarter. Transformation! Every café jammed, the streets dense with people, windows brightly lit. I stop every 10 yards, either to take a leaflet or buy an amateurishly printed student paper, or to drop a coin in a collection-tin for medical aid, or to listen to one of the countless impromptu discussions that attract knots of students in the roadway. Not a cop to be seen: on the Boulevard St Michel, students with armbands control the traffic, clear a path for an occasional car with *'Serrez s'il vous plaît, camarades!'* This is the republic of free Paris, the community of living ideas and exploding hopes, the *de facto* independent state which someone calls 'our revolutionary Vatican'.

Signs of battle? The stumps of sawn trees, asphalt freshly laid (a permanent improvement) where paving-stones had been torn up, a few kiosks burned out by police grenades. But seldom a single broken window, seldom a damaged building. Throughout the troubles there wasn't even a hint of looting, barely a single petty theft: student patrols were on the watch, and anyway no one thought of it. Local people laugh or reply with outraged denials to the stories of 'the underworld', of 'anarchy', disseminated in unison by the authorities and the communist press. Bookshops, sandwich-bars and chemists are open late into the night.

I push my way into the Sorbonne. The vast courtyard is filled with the same endlessly talking groups. Total tolerance is the unbroken rule; Maoists offer their intellectual wares side by side with upholders of Yugoslav self-management, Trotskyists with anarchists, Zionists with advocates of Arab liberation. Victor Hugo presides benevolently, red flag strapped to his stone hand.

The young men are intense but strangely calm with a fine inner confidence; eyes red from sleepless nights, but mostly with freshly shaven cheeks or trimmed beards. The girls are lovely with their pale faces, long hair, big serious eyes, and those who aren't intrinsically beautiful are rendered beautiful by their faith and their vivacity. Love is incorporated into discussion by means of squeezed hands and rapid kisses. A pair of militant lesbians, both dazzling, embrace boldly.

Tuesday morning: I go to the Ecole des Beaux Arts in search of the revolutionary posters that were being sold 'for the struggle', but collectors have cleaned up already. Notices on the doors announce 'Bicycle bureau'; 'Petrol for ambulances collected here'; 'Blood donors'; 'Clothes washed cleaned and lent (modern styles)'. In the university there's more work being done than in a normal academic year. Architects are busy on the problem of building accidents due to hasty construction for the sake of profit. Sociologists are collecting evidence for a future White Book on police atrocities (I read a few statements and feel sick). Last night a conference of 1,600 people from all levels of the film industry worked out a reform plan.

I spend two hours in the occupied Odéon Theatre, *'tribune libre'* for day and night discussion. An African student is holding forth about the problems of the third world. Some impatience from those pre-occupied with French events; a voice demands, *'De quelle révolution s'agit-il?'* Another voice replies: *'Du monde!'* Everyone cheers. Then a man who says he's a worker declares that he doesn't care about the underdeveloped countries. A girl gesticulates: 'But you live on them! Do you take sugar in coffee?' A building foreman urges student-worker unity, remarks that he's never been in this theatre before but he likes it. A girl answers: 'I'd never been in the Renault works till last week but I liked that too.'

Wednesday was the day of breathless hope, when De Gaulle left Paris and it seemed magically possible that he was abandoning power. The communists and the CGT staged an immense demonstration, marching from the Place de la Bastille to the heart of 'respectable' Paris. Half an hour after the first contingents moved off, others were waiting to get into the huge Place; I watched a group of youngsters dancing the Carmagnole and singing the revolutionary songs that are the Frenchman's inheritance. For the first time anyone can remember, the communist *service d'ordre* had to allow Maoist and Trotskyist groups to join in under their own banners – absolutely no discord or bad feeling about this.

On Thursday came the counter-attack. De Gaulle's broadcast caught me in the barber's chair. It didn't scare anyone – the barber remarked: 'He wants to die like a hero' – but soon there were signs of the mobilisation of Gaullist shock-troops. Cars draped in *tricolores* (and mysteriously full of petrol) raced along Boulevard St Germain blowing their horns and trying to provoke trouble. Later, I was to find the Champs Elysées blocked solid with them after midnight, all tooting the *'Algérie Française'* rhythm.

At six I went to watch the Gaullist demonstration along the Champs

Elysées. Stopping in a café to make a phone call, I heard the man ahead of me say: 'Darling? I'm just going to march for a bit – bring the car to collect me at the Etoile.' The crowd was certainly huge; I don't think it was bigger than the CGT's, but beyond a certain point estimates become guesses. Almost entirely well-dressed, inclined to be elderly, people unused to this kind of action and enjoying it in the manner of American businessmen at a college reunion or an American Legion spree. Chants of *'La France au travail', 'Nettoyez la Sorbonne', 'Cest nous la majorité!'* The strangest thing was to see US-owned firms with *tricolores* all over their balconies and cheered by the marchers.

But the demonstration had an ugly side. The jingo, xenophobic slogan of *'La France aux Français!'* – a traditional classic of the Right – was often heard. So was another old favourite: *'La police avec nous!'* The shout which I didn't hear myself, but which was well attested enough to be reported in *Le Monde*, was *'Cohn-Bendit à Dachau!'* That night an Italian friend went to the cinema; when Cohn-Bendit appeared in the newsreel there were cries of *'Au four!'* (To the crematorium). On the march I saw plenty of faces – mostly the well-powdered faces of ladies in hats – distorted with hatred and the hunger for revenge. A contingent of nuns was yelling 'Mitterrand in prison!' Setting the picture beside that of the day before, I saw the eternal *'deux Frances'* – sans-culottes and aristos, Commune and Versailles. The enemy is still Shelley's: 'old Custom, legal Crime, and bloody Faith'.

Back to the Sorbonne late in the evening. A student was speaking through a loud-hailer: 'It's the time of double power. Organise your action committees everywhere, organise the power of the workers by hand and brain!' But nobody was organising. The two great boulevards of the Quarter were thicker than ever before with chattering groups; our Speakers' Corner multiplied by fifty, except that there were no speakers and listeners, only the immense harmony of the endless discussion. One never had a sense of defeat, but one did have a sense of unreality as the vital hours trickled away. There were people enough – and to spare – to set up a rival government, to take and garrison a stronghold like the Hôtel de Ville. But the hard logic remains: you don't make a revolution without leadership, without a revolutionary party. The Party didn't want revolution, those who wanted revolution had no party. Simple.

I waited in a Left Bank flat to meet two committee members of Cohn-Bendit's '22 March Movement'. They had phoned at midnight to say they had responsibilities, they'd be a bit late. Finally we talked from half past one to three. The boy was whiplash-lean and intense, but that side of him somehow co-existed with charm, wit, even a certain elegance. The girl – another of those pale beauties – fixed her dark eyes on me and assured me that there was nothing to be depressed about. 'Could we have taken power? But that's not what it's all about; we want to break up power, not to transfer it.'

Friday was a dead day: a general feeling of weariness, a return to normal – with the holiday weekend ahead, motorists spent hours queueing at the reopened petrol stations – and an exchange of rumours and theories about what had really happened behind the scenes. The weather, fine all the week, became suddenly hot. Tourist Paris began to revive.

On Saturday the Students' Union held its defiant demonstration. Boycotted once more by the communists, dismissed as pointless folly or crazy adventurism by many well-wishers, it nevertheless mustered a good 30,000 marchers. I join in near the head of the column, behind the proudly waving red and black flags. I've never marched under anarchist colours before, but what the hell. Students are laughing at the *Humanité* report of a speech by Waldeck-Rochet: 'Our flags are not those of anarchy but the red flag of socialism and the *tricolore*, the flag of the nation.' But this week the *tricolore* and the Marseillaise belong to De Gaulle; they've never been so clearly the symbols of conservatism. We pass a school adorned like all French schools with its obligatory *tricolore*. The caretaker first waves to the marchers, then clambers out on the balcony, seizes the flag, and methodically tears away the blue and white segments. '*Ça y est, camarade!*'

We shout '*Etudiants travailleurs solidaires!*', '*À bas l'état des patrons!*', '*Révolution socialiste!*' '*Elections-trahison!*' And the slogan coined as a retort to the expulsion of Cohn-Bendit: '*Nous sommes tous des juifs allemands*'. ('Not very plausible in my case, but never mind,' remarks an African.) And, again and again: '*Ce n'est qu'un début, continuons le combat!*' The spirit is marvellous, full of determination and courage and always that special French gaiety. The marchers are of all social classes, maybe with a predominance of white-collar workers, technicians, teachers, but with some banners from factories too. The common denominator is youth; hardly anyone is over 40. Talking to marchers, I begin to understand the clarity of thought, the real maturity of this movement. There are no illusions; we all know that De Gaulle has won this round of the struggle. But we're marching because it's necessary to guard the fighting spirit, to refute in advance the myths sure to be spread in the coming weeks: the Gaullist myth of restored national unity, the communist myth that the movement was declining. The student beside me tucks her hair into her red kerchief, links arms with me again, and tells me calmly: 'Yes, of course it's all over now.' Then she starts shouting again: '*Ce n'est qu'un début . . .*'

Circling round the Left Bank from Montparnasse, we end up by the Austerlitz station and shout to the pickets of railwaymen: *'La grève continue! – Ne signez pas!'* They wave back, give us the clenched fist salute, join in the International. We sit down in the roadway and hear some short speeches; greetings from an Italian student get a special cheer. Finally we're urged to make our way to Citroën and Renault and 'discuss' with the workers.

That night the police were back in the Quarter: a score of buses and camionettes drawn up outside Lipp's, the men wary and anxious, far less cheerful than the students even in their hour of victory. It's all over – and it isn't. The stories of apathy, of the 'depoliticisation' of French youth, of contentment and conformity are refuted for ever. Revolutionary France is reborn. *Ce n'est qu'un début.*

Spectator, 12 July 1968   *Tibor Szamuely*

THE CANCEROUS SOCIETY

Many years ago, at a Soviet Communist party conference, the party secretary of Tula Region, reporting on the splendid cultural progress of his satrapy, proudly announced that the number of writers there had increased forty-two times over since the revolution: now there were forty-two writers working in Tula Region whereas in backward tsarist days it had possessed only one solitary representative of the literary profession – Leo Tolstoy.

This statement is fairly typical of the Soviet Union, where literary progress, like the production of steel ingots or petrol or shoes, is measured almost solely in terms of quantity. At last year's Writers' Congress speakers constantly repeated the proud boast: 'The Soviet Union has more writers than any other country in the world.' All perfectly true: there are even probably more certified writers in the USSR than in all the rest of the world put together. Perhaps even more than in the whole previous history of mankind. Think of it: in May 1967 there were 6,608 writers in Russia, all neatly classified into the appropriate categories of prose-writers, poets, playwrights and critics.

There is only one drawback to this creative paradise, namely that all 6,608 do not add up to a single Tolstoy. In fact, in any other country no more than a dozen or so out of these serried masses of pen-pushers would be regarded as writers at all. For in their infinite solicitude for the moral well-being of the Soviet people the Communist party has, over the past fifty years, gone to great lengths to weed out any author of talent, integrity and independence. By a variety of means – execution, prison camp, suicide, or simply non-publication – the desired result, the murder of a great literary tradition, has been effected in full measure.

In recent years, however, what with the deplorable laxity of the security police, the watchdogs of literary orthodoxy have run into difficulties. Some of these have now been happily eliminated, and the culprits put behind bars. But Soviet literature has by no means been restored to its customary tranquillity of the graveyard. The main reason for this disturbing state of affairs has been the appearance in Russia, after a lapse of twenty or thirty years, of a genuine novelist of the first rank: Alexander Solzhenitsyn.

What makes Solzhenitsyn different from the other 6,607 is not just his immense talent – that could be forgiven, however grudgingly – but his adamant resolve to write the truth and nothing but the truth: to describe what life in the Land of Socialism is really like. One subject above all personally concerns every single Soviet citizen regardless of class, race, creed or social position, a subject that had never ever been hinted at in public: the purges and the slave-labour camps. Alexander Solzhenitsyn is the man who first told his people the truth about the communist inferno – and who has gone on telling it.

Solzhenitsyn erupted on the Soviet literary scene in November 1962 with the publication – authorised by a majority decision of Khrushchev's Politburo – of *One Day in the Life of Ivan Denisovich*. Never before has an author had such instantaneous success: Solzhenitsyn became world-famous overnight. The publication of *Ivan Denisovich* was not only the greatest Soviet literary occasion in a generation, but also the most important political event since Khruschev's 1956 Secret Speech. In one short novelette Solzhenitsyn laid bare the black horror at the heart of Soviet society, the existence of a vast system of human slavery.

After having spent eight years in the camps, Solzhenitsyn knew all about them – as did countless millions of his fellow-countrymen. He described a typical camp day in 1951; it so happens that at that precise time I was myself in a camp of the same type, situated in a similar locality. I am therefore in a position to vouch for the accuracy of every hideous detail in Solzhenitsyn's book. But, of course, it is only western readers, fed for years on the soothing pap of fellow-travelling lies, who need confirmation of the truth: no Russian ever doubted it for a moment. They knew that this was what it was like – only they had never seen it mentioned in print before.

For months people could talk of little else but *Ivan Denisovich*. The literary establishment, the party hacks and the police informers, had to grind their teeth impotently and hope for better times. Meanwhile Solzhenitsyn, a reserved and retiring man living quietly in the provincial town of Ryazan, became the idol of the new generation of 'unofficial' writers which suddenly sprung up throughout the country. The monlithic unity of Soviet literature was at an end, and even some of the older writers began remembering words and concepts which they had known in their youth and had tried to forget for many years – like 'honesty,' 'courage,' 'dignity,' 'decency.'

It did not take long for the party to realise the danger. With Khrushchev and his un-Bolshevik fits of petty-bourgeois sentimentality safely out of the way, the new tough party leadership (quaintly known as 'liberal' in some western circles) decided to strike – hard. First Sinyavsky and Daniel, then other groups of underground writers, then their sympathisers: happy days were here again for the copper's narks of the Union of Soviet Writers. And now, the preliminary work being done, they are ready to demolish the man whom they, and the party leadership, hate more than anyone else, the one great living writer of the USSR, Alexander Solzhenitsyn. The publication a fortnight ago in *Literaturnaya Gazeta* of a long and uncommonly vicious unsigned attack upon Solzhenitsyn marks the beginning of the open campaign, the inception of the biggest Soviet literary row since the Pasternak affair ten years ago.

The systematic harassment of Solzhenitsyn has actually been going on for more than three years. First they stopped publishing him; then his writings were removed from the libraries and all mention of his name prohibited; then his home was searched by the police and his manuscripts and archives confiscated. Foul rumours were put about by the authorities: that he had been a traitor in the war, that he had attempted to establish a terroristic organisation, that he was mad, and so on. Finally, goaded beyond all endurance, Solzhenitsyn sent an open letter to the delegates of the Fourth Writers' Congress (which, needless to say, he had not been invited to attend). Solzhenitsyn did not limit himself to protesting against his own persecution: he boldly called for the complete abolition of censorship, 'of the oppression, insupportable in the long run, to which our literature has for decades and decades been subjected on the part of the censorship.'

Officially no cognizance was taken of Solzhenitsyn's letter. But in the changed political climate of the Soviet Union many delegates, sick to the heart for having remained silent too long, registered their shock and indignation. The distinguished poet Antokolsky wrote to Demichev, Secretary of the Central Committee: 'If Solzhenitsyn cannot say what he wants to say to the readers in our country then I, an old writer, have no right to face the readers either.' He was not alone: seventy-nine signed a petition calling for an open discussion of Solzhenitsyn's letter. They were told that this was out of the question.

As the months passed Solzhenitsyn continued to press for the publication of his works – and warned that otherwise some of them would inevitably appear abroad. The authorities were clearly at a loss: on the one hand they negotiated with Solzhenitsyn regarding possible emendations – while at the same time the editor of *Pravda*, Zimyanin, issued a violent verbal attack against the novelist at a meeting of journalists, calling him a schizophrenic who 'finds only sores and cancerous tumours' in Soviet society, and concluding that 'obviously we cannot publish his works.'

Having now read the manuscripts of two of Solzhenitsyn's novels, shortly to be published in English – Part One of *The Cancer Ward*, and *In the First Circle* – I can well understand why the Soviet government could never permit their publication in Russia. These are not only great works of literature: they reveal communist society from the inside, in all its cruelty and corruption, its inhumanity and injustice. Here is a terrifying picture – but it also contains hope; hope and faith in the indomitable nature of man, capable of preserving his humanity through physical and moral hells undreamed-of by writers or theologians of past ages.

The action of *The Cancer Ward* takes place in February 1955 in (obviously) the cancer ward of a hospital in Central Asia. (Solzhenitsyn himself spent many months after his release in a Tashkent hospital undergoing treatment for a malignant tumour.) At first we learn all about the patients' medical symptoms and diagnoses – then gradually, as we get to know them one by one, we begin to discover that the malignant cancer of Soviet society, which had warped their souls and ruined their lives, transformed them into heartless informers and dehumanised ex-convicts, into careerists and drudges, is a far more terrible disease than the tumours rotting their bodies and gradually killing them off. *The Cancer Ward* is the Soviet Union.

In the First Circle is too vast a novel – over 200,000 words, with a cast of characters ranging from Stalin to semi-literate convicts – even to attempt to describe in brief. The title is taken from Dante: the first, comparatively most lenient circle of Inferno – in this case one of those peculiar Soviet institutions, a scientific institute run by the MGB and staffed by convict scientists engaged in inventing and producing technical devices for trapping and convicting other people. They lead a relatively privileged existence – but they are still convicts; they receive white bread while their bosses and overseers get Stalin Prizes for their inventions. This, in fact, is how much of the 'great Soviet achievement' that we hear about so often was really brought about – by slaves. Cheops + cybernetics = Soviet power, if one may paraphrase a famous slogan of Lenin's.

No wonder the communist establishment is baying for Solzhenitsyn's blood. *Literaturnaya Gazeta* calls him an anti-Soviet renegade, compares him with Svetlana Alliluyeva,* accuses him of cooperating with 'reactionary Western Propaganda.' As for *In the First Circle*: 'rabid slander of our social system.'

In the Soviet Union such accusations usually lead to grave consequences, to put it mildly. But what can they do to Solzhenitsyn? He has already been through it all, and hell hath no terrors for him any more. *In the First Circle* contains his reply, in the form of a convict-engineer's brusque retort to Abakumov, the dreaded Minister of State Security (in 1949):

'I have nothing left, do you understand – nothing! You can't get at my wife and child – a bomb got them. My parents are dead. All my worldly property is a handkerchief, my boiler suit and my buttonless linen belong to the state. You've taken away my freedom a long time ago, and you can't return it because you haven't got any yourself. I'm forty-two, you sentenced me to twenty-five years; I've been on hard labour, and done time in the punishment cells, and worn handcuffs, and been guarded by dogs, and been in a punitive brigade – what else can you threaten me with? You're only strong while you haven't taken *everything* away. But a man from whom you've taken *everything* is no longer compliant to your will. He is free again.'

Alexander Solzhenitsyn has been through many circles of the communist Hell, and as a result he is today a free citizen of a cancerous society. This makes him such a difficult customer to handle. And there are very many more in the same position. This, I believe, is known as the law of diminishing returns.

New Statesman, 31 January 1969   *Kingsley Martin*

GANDHI: A PERSONAL ASSESSMENT

Today, exactly 21 years after his assassination, the Establishment pays homage to Mahatma Gandhi, who for more than a generation successfully rebelled against the British Raj. A service at St Paul's with an oration by the archbishop would have brought an ironic chuckle

* Better known as Svetlana Stalin – K.A.

from the Mahatma. If the British bar, which once expelled him as a jailbird, decides to reinstate him posthumously, he will become a respectable British personality. When we buy a stamp bearing his portrait we are unlikely to remember that he meditated serenely in British jails for some 2,500 days and that Churchill described him as a 'naked fakir'. The Indians have long ago turned him into a saint. In this country we follow a familiar pattern; we persecute the rebel during his life; when he is dead and no longer dangerous we canonise him and forget what he taught.

I suppose that insofar as people in this country recall his teaching at all, they think of him simply as a pacifist. This is a misleading picture. Amongst other things he was a successful barrister with a shrewd and realistic mind and a gay, vivacious sense of humour. He only gradually evolved his theory of non-violence after he had discovered in South Africa what it was like to be a coloured man. He learnt that it was possible to maintain his dignity as a human being and to win political battles though he was insulted and beaten up. He rejected the doctrine that England's predicament was India's opportunity, and in the Boer War, clad in khaki and puttees, he served in an ambulance unit and attained the rank of sergeant-major. In 1914 he still held that, when England was in danger, it was a duty to serve the government which he had accepted in time of peace. He even recruited for the army. But by that time he had become the spokesman of all Indians in South Africa and had won for the Indian community a complete, if temporary, victory. He had bargained with General Smuts and earned his admiration. His doctrine of Satyagraha had taken shape and definition. As a theory it owed much to the New Testament as well as the Gita, and the modern authors who contributed to it were Thoreau, Tolstoy and Ruskin. He had proved before his final return to India in 1915 that the weak are not necessarily powerless.

Satyagraha is a composite word meaning 'firmness for truth'. It was, Gandhi held, the 'most active form of resistance'; it involved a resolute assertion of what one believed right, maintained without violence or compromise whatever violence was used against one. Real victory consists in persuading your opponent that you are right; to convert him is to triumph. Such an attitude must never be confused with cowardice; he said repeatedly that rather than run away because you are frightened, it is better to fight.

In order to discipline himself as a Satyagrahist he discarded not only all the pleasures, but what most people would regard as the necessities of life. Goat's milk was permitted; because of the cruel treatment of cows, cow's milk was rejected. How far could he live on fruit and lemon juice? He would spend years before making a vow, but having made it he would maintain it to the point of death. He told his wife that he must altogether refrain from sexual intercourse, and recorded that twice he failed to control his passion. I wrote recently that his wife resented his abstinence; in fact he says that she accepted his vow without demur. My mistake arose from recalling how he infuriated her by other demands; he decided, for instance, that all the personal jewellery she was given in gratitude for their services in Africa must be discarded. He treated her roughly and believed that a Hindu husband had absolute rights over his wife. It was one of his peculiarities that he admitted his lapses and was always ready to do penance for his own and also other people's sins. It was this latter atonement for others which most puzzled the Western mind.

His idea that the British would grant India freedom after she had fought for them in the 1914 war was shattered by the atrocious events at Amritsar, when nearly 400 Indians were shot in cold blood, not to prevent them from breaking the law, but, as General Dyer explained, as 'a punishment'. Floggings and the 'crawling order' were the last indignities: they brought Gandhi into active politics. Clearly India had to fight for her freedom, though fight, in his definition, meant resist by Satyagraha. Hundreds of young Indians accepted the challenge and lay down in the road presenting themselves without weapons to be beaten by police *lathis*. In this fight Gandhi won moral victories but suffered many disappointments. There were occasions on which the crowd following him resorted to force and even committed atrocities on the police. Gandhi would then proclaim a fast against his own followers. They would be penitent and terrified lest he should die and the British authorities were also frightened of the revolutionary effects which might follow his death.

He made a profound impression on Lord Reading when he was Viceroy and also on Lord Irwin and, perhaps most remarkable of all, on the judge who tried him for a seditious article in *Young India*. His speech before sentence on that occasion is one of the most notable ever made in a court of law. He gave a full account of British cruelty and repression which justified his article. He then went on to state that the prosecution's case had been put perfectly fairly, and that he did not ask for mercy or plead any extenuating circumstances. 'The only course open to you, the judge,' he said, 'is either to resign your post or to inflict on me the severest penalty, if you believe that the system and the law you administer are good for the people.' The judge and the prisoner bowed to each other; the judge said: 'Even those who differ from you in politics look upon you as a man of high ideals and of noble and even

saintly life.' He sent Gandhi to jail for six years, saying how pleased he
would be if the government would reduce the term.

No one could doubt that Gandhi had learnt personally to accept
violence without returning it. But this is only the beginning of the
problem of Satyagraha. What is the non-violent resister to do when not
he, but those whom he is expected to defend, are attacked? The answer
which he gave to a well-known Negro minister who, with his wife, paid
Gandhi a visit was surely unsatisfying. Mrs Thurman asked Gandhi the
crucial question. 'How am I to act, supposing my own brother is
lynched before my very eyes?' His reply was confused. The answer
which came to him, he said, was that 'he must not wish ill to the
lynchers, but neither must he cooperate with them! It may be that
ordinarily I depend upon the lynching community for my livelihood. I
refuse to cooperate with them, refuse even to touch food that comes
from them and I refuse to cooperate with even my brother Negroes who
tolerate the wrong.' He added that he did not expect to convince Mrs
Thurman, 'but I am striving very hard; even if I do not succeed fully in
this life my faith is undiminished.'

'Do I contradict myself?' he asked. 'Consistency is a hobgoblin.' He
was doing his best, as he told Mrs Thurman, and in many issues of
Harijan he discussed the difficulties of Satyagraha. It is often forgotten
that Gandhi was a journalist whose distinction was to show the
weakness as well as the strength of his arguments. Nowhere was he less
clear than on the issue of Japan's expected invasion of India. The
British were still ruling India, but everywhere retreating before the
triumphant Japanese. Congress was divided and many were ready to
aid the Japanese in throwing out the British. Gandhi's own formula was
'not to put any obstacle in the way of the British forces'. That is, it was
not India's business to assist the British actively, but to offer complete
passive resistance to the Japanese. Non-violent behaviour towards
aggressive Japan meant not to give food or shelter or have any dealings
with the invaders. He explained this in *Harijan*, adding 'it was
superstition to imagine that the Japanese would come as "friendlies". If
the people cannot resist fierce attack and are afraid of death, they must
evacuate the infected place in order to deny compulsory service to the
enemy.' Realising that such remarks made an inadequate programme
for dealing with the Japanese, he discussed how India after victory
would be morally bound to help the democratic nations against
Fascism.

Three days before his assassination I had a long talk with Gandhi
about the use of force by the government in power. Did not a
government use force by its very nature? I recalled the actual situation

in Kashmir. India had fought to prevent the Muslim tribesmen
destroying Srinagar as they already had Baramullah. In order to avoid
future conflict and the development of war, should not India accept the
ceasefire line as a permanent division between Indian and Pakistan-
occupied Kashmir? He was quite cross. He said I was only a journalist.
I had not read the documents and had no right to make such proposals.
I was somewhat abashed but, since Gandhi was always candid, he
added that he no doubt felt rather strongly on the subject because two
very well-informed persons had made the same suggestion to him
during the previous week. I felt that perhaps I was not such a fool after
all. The two well-informed persons were Rajagopalachari, the next
Governor-General of India, and the then Governor-General, Lord
Mountbatten, who told me that he had argued with Gandhi on this
point and parted in strong disagreement with him only a few days
before.

Gandhi fought unceasingly for Indian independence, but he put first
the manner in which she gained it and the sort of state that a free India
would be. He did not wish India to gain independence by force and he
demanded that she should first cure her own faults. He infuriated
many Indian nationalists by saying that Indians did not deserve
independence. She must not imitate the follies of western civilisation.
The spinning wheel was a symbol of independence; if Indians made
their own homespun, they would not be in debt to Lancashire. He was
not opposed to machinery, and did not deny that scientific discoveries
and inventions might benefit mankind. But he believed that their
influence was wholly bad if they led to western pleasure-seeking, to
greed of possession, and the accumulation of wealth. He was no
advocate of poverty; indeed he believed it was as destructive of the
good life as riches. The attainable goal was to lessen desire; if you
learnt to be satisfied with a minimum, you might become impervious
both to bribes and threats.

Gandhi's attitude to the Hindu scriptures was very similar to Christ's
towards the Old Testament. Indians had ceased to study the *Vedas*;
they took for granted that there was moral value in their stories of
bloodshed and violence. Gandhi read the opening passages of the *Gita*
as a summons to Satyagraha and, like Jesus Christ, who could quote
Jewish history to support a new morality, he wrote what amounted to a
new interpretation of Hinduism. It was to him terrible that such
customs as child marriage, of which he himself was a victim, should
continue in India and that millions of his fellow countrymen should be
regarded as 'untouchable'. Perhaps there is nothing in the Mahatma's
career more worthy than his deliberate acceptance of equality with the

Untouchables; his *ashram* nearly broke up when he brought Untouchables into its membership and made it clear that the cleaning of lavatories and the sweeping up of filth were part of a caste Hindu's normal duties.

Speaking about the Untouchables, Gandhi once said:

If we, the Indians have become the outcasts of empire, it is retributive justice meted out to us by a just god. Should we Hindus not wash our bloodstained hands before we ask the English to wash theirs? Untouchability has degraded us, made us into outcasts. So long as Hindus regard untouchability as part of their religion, so long is freedom impossible of attainment. India is guilty. England has done nothing blacker and we are not better than brutes until we have purged ourselves of the sins we have committed against our weaker brethren.

Untouchability was, and is today, India's racial problem. The first onslaught upon it was made by Gandhi; the fact that Untouchables now play their part in every sphere of Indian life is the result of Gandhi's example. It takes many years before any prejudice as deep as that against untouchability can be altogether overcome. And there are still religious Hindus who have not outlived the deep-rooted habit of treating Untouchables as animals. But to Gandhi they were Harijans, the 'people of God'.

India to Gandhi was one. He never accepted partition. The creation of Pakistan was to him a catastrophe. When he said, not long before his death, that he was a 'spent bullet', he surely referred to his failure to overcome communal hostility. In January 1948 he made a largely successful effort to end the terrible massacres in Calcutta and on 13 January he began a fast that was likely to continue till death in order to make Delhi again a civilised town. It had become unsafe for any Muslim to walk the streets of the Indian capital. He only abandoned his fast five days later when he received the pledge from a wide circle of Hindu society to end hostility towards Muslims. It was more than a documentary pledge. He waited for definite evidence that Muslim refugees could return to Delhi and that joint Hindu–Muslim activities were being prepared for the future.

I myself saw him next when he held a prayer meeting at Mehrauli, a Muslim sanctuary which had been looted by fanatical Hindus. The followers of Islam dared to return to their own place of worship. I was amongst them in the crowd when Gandhi arrived; he saw me and beckoned to me to sit by his side while he held the service. That was the last occasion on which I saw him. Two days later, at his prayer meeting at Birla House, he was shot by a Hindu fanatic who charged him with the crime of being friendly to the Muslim community. It was his influence that induced Patel to pay over monies which were due to Pakistan and it was by his influence that the mosques were again opened and were safe for Muslims.

People often talk as if Gandhi's non-violence was by itself responsible for Britain's withdrawal from India. It is true that the national movement was canalised into comparatively orderly and peaceful channels by Gandhi; he was worshipped as a symbol of Hindu nationalism and venerated by almost all the vast Indian population. He aroused it from apathy and endowed it with purpose. There were special reasons for his success. The British were embarrassed by the technique of non-violence and Labour had voted for India's independence for generations. A large body of British opinion was ashamed to see non-resisting, helpless people beaten down by police and soldiers when their only crime was to demand the self-government they had long been promised. But it was to Attlee's credit that he saw that the time had come when he must cut through the many obstacles to Indian independence even at the cost of partition. He was certainly supported by expert civil and military advice and realised that Britain would become involved in a prolonged and dishonouring war if she again failed to grant India independence.

Too much and too little is claimed for non-violence. Some will say that it can achieve moral victory even when it ends in physical disaster. After all, violent fighting for a good cause may be unsuccessful and in any case it will leave behind it even after victory the seeds of future conflict. In circumstances like those of India, Satyagraha certainly achieved success where violence would have failed. Non-violence is understood in the East far better than in the West but the British were democratic and sensitive to world opinion. On the other hand, no one will argue that non-violence would have stopped the Japanese if they had invaded India. Today, many people finding less and less satisfaction in violent demonstrations, are talking of the hopeful use of Satyagraha. Its value still has to be tested in the racial struggle, which is probably the most important cause in world politics today. How far the non-violent movement in America can survive the murder of Martin Luther King, Gandhi's greatest disciple, remains an open question.

New Statesman, 14 November 1969   *C. H. Rolph*
THE HANGMEN FIGHT BACK

Whether we keep the death penalty for murder or abolish it, two things are likely to remain unchanged. One is the murder rate in this country and the other is the insatiable British appetite for talking angrily about God's law and 'the supreme punishment'. In this country as in no other, the vast demands of television programming have turned the death-penalty controversy into a branch of the entertainment industry, played in and out to comic signature tunes and a shouting audience. Wherever else in the world you go, you find that most countries where it has been abolished (and that means most countries) have virtually forgotten it. The exceptions are those where they annually publish detailed 'criminal statistics' which (like ours) are uniformly impossible to interpret and which, whatever they disclose, are used by each side to confound the other.

Nevertheless to ignore the figures altogether would be irresponsible; and a valid but strangely muted abolitionist argument is that if the figures were really significant – if abolition sent up the annual murders from, say, their present 160 to something like 10,000 – then there would be no controversy. There might still be those who would not support the taking of a life whatever the reason and who would, one supposes, see the human race extinguished by one maniac rather than have him killed. They can be left to their moral dilemma: no man can resolve it for them. The publication of the long-awaited report on post-abolition murder figures by the Home Office Research Unit has shown once again that murder rates cannot be tied to any form of murder penalty, and yet it will be those figures rather than the moral absolutes that should inform the coming debates in Parliament. In December the government will introduce resolutions in both Houses to prolong (indefinitely?) the life of the Murder (Abolition of Death Penalty) Act 1965 beyond 31 July 1970, its provisional date of expiry. Someone will probably challenge the government's view of section 4 of the Act, which says:

This Act shall continue in force until 31 July 1970 and shall then expire, *unless* Parliament by affirmative resolutions of both Houses otherwise determines.

What does the word 'unless' relate to? The continuing in force or the expiry? This is not by any means a frivolous question. There seems little doubt that Parliament meant the 'affirmative resolutions' to be concerned with expiry on 31 July and to come up for debate then, not to decide six months in advance that the Act be given a new lease.

The newly published murder rate is still insignificant by comparison, for example, with America's. Ours remains as it has been for many years, a rate of three per million of the population 'at risk'. (The Home Office excludes, by this phrase 'at risk', children under eight. It is an odd phrase, because the statistical 'risk' is not that they would have been murdered but that they would have murdered others. The age at which a child can now be charged with a crime is 10, but it was seven from 1908 to 1933 and eight from then until 1963; and eight is retained as convenient for the needs of long-term statistical comparison.) Parallels with America can be only approximate, for a number of statistical and semantic reasons, but they are startling enough to survive all scepticism.

In 1967, according to *The Times* New York Correspondent, New York City had a murder rate of 96 per million – and its policemen prided themselves that this was the lowest in the 10 largest American cities. The highest was 260 per million in Houston, Texas. Our own three per million looks modest enough in that setting? In their forthcoming book *The Honest Politician's Guide to Crime Control*, Norval Morris and Gordon Hawkins quote the FBI's 'Uniform Crime Reports'. These started in 1949 and their heading 'Murder and Non-Negligent Manslaughter' covers all intentional criminal killings *known to the police*. In 1949 the US murder rate according to these was 52 per million, in 1966 it was 56 and in 1967 it was 61. It had dropped to 40 in 1957. Even the current rates are 30 per cent lower than in 1933, according to unpublished figures held by the FBI; and 'the hysteria in the press and on television about murder rates,' write Morris and Hawkins, 'is thus historically unfounded'. It might be going too far to say that Mr Duncan Sandys's supporters are hysterical over here, but how long would it take them to succumb in, say, Houston, where the death penalty flourishes side by side with a murder rate of 260 per million?

What should worry our abolitionists more than it does is their own supporters' ingrained habit of claiming that the death penalty is 'no deterrent'. What they surely mean is that it is only one of several and that we ought, for reasons of decency, to give it up and try one of the others. Every penalty deters somebody, though neither the threat of death nor anything else will deter a killer who proposes to commit suicide after the crime, or who is insane. Hangers are equally rash in declaring that imprisonment is 'no deterrent', since the figures usually remain unchanged whether you hang or imprison.

Better grounded is the worry about prolonged imprisonment. Not because a man is 'destroyed' by prison after about 10 years – in modern conditions that is just not true, for I know men who have served much longer sentences and are far from destroyed; but the public are likely always – or for a very long time – to feel that 'murder' (which they don't qualify) is the supreme crime and that 30-year sentences for robbers must somehow be matched by even greater ferocity for murderers. The answer will eventually be to lower the temperature about robbers, but meanwhile the judges have set themselves a pattern that it will be difficult not to follow until violent crime begins to fall.

When will that be? Since the 'increase' in violent crime may be largely a statistical phenomenon, and our statistical methods are producing a progressively clearer picture of something that has been going on without our knowledge, it will not be for many years. I believe that if we suddenly knew the true extent of theft and sex offences, for example, hysteria would really be the word. We shall get to know gradually, with annual crises that will sometimes rock governments. Then one day we shall know the computerised worst; murder will be seen to have stayed where it was; and even Mr Sandys, if he's still there, will be glad we did not after all rebuild our prison gallows and snatch back those prison recreation rooms that used to be condemned cells.

Spectator, 13 June 1970   *George Gale*
THE STYLE OF HAROLD WILSON

Many years ago, when it was one of my obligations to visit the Marquis of Granby – a public house beside Transport House, then the headquarters of the Labour party, the TUC and the T&GW – in order to find out what the members of the national executive of the Labour party and of the General Council of the TUC were saying about each other and about the affairs of the day (usually in that order), I sometimes would check up later with one of those members of the national executive who tended not to drink in the Marquis of Granby.

I was working for the *Manchester Guardian*, and I would check up with someone who was once, somewhat earlier, turned down for a job there. He having come on and up in the world a bit since, but retaining that kind of fond affection and respect combined with superior despair that most men who've done well feel towards those who once dispensed with their services, was invariably nice to me. This is not my point. He was also invariably honest; and this I have not forgotten.

By honest, I mean what I say. I would sometimes ring him up and ask him what had happened and often he would tell me that he could not say. Other times he would tell me that I had it wrong, or right, as the case might be. Occasionally he would tell me what had happened – not, of course, the whole truth about what had happened, but, so far as I was able subsequently to tell, nothing but the truth. He never, so far as I knew, gave me a bum steer. Since then I have followed the career of that member of the national executive with as much interest as anyone else and, at times, with more sympathy than most. There have been many times since then when I have suspected him of giving Lobby journalists a bum steer, but not being of the Lobby, nor by nature clement towards its inbred methods and its more bumptious members, I have felt tolerant towards him in anything he may have done in this direction: it being, I think, legitimate to give Lobby correspondents a bum steer if you can think of nothing better, or different, to do, on, say, a thin Friday in March. I mean, what else are some Lobby fodder for? Let them eat bum steers. There are, as Harold Wilson might say (and indeed did on Monday morning, in not all that different a context), some very honourable exceptions to the rule.

It is, of course, of Harold Wilson that I speak, or sing. Of whom else? He has bestrode this election like a cosy pet and cuddly toy Colossus. I cannot contemplate his performance without wishing to break into hoots of laughter; and laughter chiefly with him, what's more: not against. It has been a very funny performance. Those with delicate stomachs have squirmed a bit at some of his more outrageous antics; but none, as yet, has thrown up. Those whose guts have suffered more in past years from swallowing the behaviour of other, lesser, politicians are strong enough to take him neat. As Ted Heath has rightly said (missing the point, alas, in saying it), nothing has been too trivial for him.

A child, just turned seven, pinched his father's pipe. The father, a political education officer turned teacher, was at hand. The child, mouth full of pipe, said 'I'm Harold Wilson'. This was on Sunday morning at Hartlepools, a north-east town distinguished for being traditionally up at the top of the unemployment table. Wilson came to Hartlepools that afternoon, and in the biggest Labour club hall in the north-east, sat down at the table by the rostrum. No sooner had he sat down than Mark Brown, the child, appeared. (He told me later he'd been told to go up. Others had it that it was his own idea.) He placed himself alongside the Prime Minister and started pretending to smoke this blasted pipe. Nor was this all. He, the child that is, despite that the sky was blue and cloudless and the afternoon excessively warm, was dressed in a miniature Gannex coat, just like the Prime Minister used to wear, when the weather in England was all cold and wet, before he started making Britain great again (or for the first time; I'm not sure, writing without all my files).

So there was this boy — I'd have said brat, except that it wasn't really his idea at all, only his father's — sitting next to the Prime Minister puffing this pipe and wearing this Gannex coat. Is nothing sacred? I sighed to myself. What does his nibs, or Wilson as the Lobby chaps call him, do next? One guess. Right. He heaves out of his jacket his pouch of baccy. Baccy, that's it. Pouch of. He says, shamelessly, 'Here you are. I'll fill your pipe for you. But don't you smoke it. Give it back to your father.' The young lad's father took the pipe and lit it, saying to me, 'You can quote me as saying "Harold's tobacco is magnificent" '; as if I'd have quoted him as saying anything else. Having stopped smoking myself a couple of years back, I thought Harold's behaviour in the worst of taste and I said this to him but he was quite unrepentant; and when I said, well, what then is the filthy shag you smoke, he said 'It's not filthy shag at all, it's a very fine tobacco. It's Rattray's of Perth, Scotland: their mixture.' Good flashy stuff, I thought, like Ted Heath and his malt scotch; none of your Bruno flake.

Following the Prime Minister around, one traipses into council house living rooms, all neat and tidy until people like us arrive, making the place look a mess, and especially the front gardens, lawns trimmed, roses ready to burst. Mary Wilson says, rightly and pleasantly, 'It must be awful, having us all come in, and even going upstairs.' There are two reasons for going upstairs, and the main one is so that Harold can lean out of the bedroom window to make a speech. At the end of the north-east tour he suddenly declares, 'Mary and I have come to a conclusion. We have been in and out of your houses, here and everywhere else. We have made a list of people's houses we have been in. We are going to invite everyone to come to our house, after the election.' To make it sure what house he means, he adds, 'Ten Downing Street is our house.' So it is. So it must remain. I cannot think that he will leave his house involuntarily. His cool, his calm, his confidence is like nothing I have ever seen from a Prime Minister (or Opposition leader) fighting an election before.

Until around February he thought he might lose; but then he suddenly knew, so he is inclined to say, that he had it made. 'The enemy is delivered into my hands.' Each day's campaigning finds him more relaxed and more at ease with his own political future. He looks ahead with pleasure, secretly telling himself, I think, that now, now will come the time, now that the economic problem of the balance of payments is manageable, now, now when he has won thrice over, will be the chance to change the place, to make the country different, to show himself to be a great Prime Minister instead of simply a successful party manager.

What other ambition, after all, can be left? Why else should he move throughout the country regally, and nicely, not having to argue the toss about this or that tedious electoral issue? Come to my home after this is all over, and I'll give you tea.

Not even Macmillan would have dared this. Macmillan, it's true, would scarcely have welcomed hundreds of house-proud Tory housewives into Downing Street; but had Macmillan thought of it, he might have gritted his teeth and borne it. Not so Harold and Mary. Mary thinks of it: not to be borne, but to be welcomed! Harold makes a little speech. Hey, ho! We have a new Queen Mum already; and a king of sorts in the offing. When Harold waves his hand, as his motorcade sweeps past, is it just my fancy that discerns a regal limpness in the gesture?

So cool and confident is this Wilson campaign that Wilson's splendid PRO – easily the best to have emerged from either political party in the many years I have followed their activities – felt it not absolutely essential to remain constantly awake during a chat the Prime Minister had with some of us on a train. Since the Prime Minister himself was stretching out his legs at the time, and obviously felt that relaxation was quite proper, there was no question of dereliction of duty. Among the topics we found ourselves discussing, in an amiable, academic kind of way, were, what the Tories should have done, what the Tories should do now, and what the Tories probably will end up doing. He is full of splendid and quite gratuitous advice.

His present technique, of breaking away from formal meetings, he regards as an overdue but very welcome break from tradition. He has had other breaks in mind. I do not think he regards manifestoes as all that much use, for instance, and election addresses, and fixed meetings. He thinks all this is traditional and nothing else: kept going, that is, because of tradition, and for no other reason. It even crossed his mind to announce a new Cabinet in the middle of the campaign. I don't say the idea stayed there for long, but it did crop up. It would have been awkward having new ministers announce answers to old ministers' problems, I think he'd allow, although since nobody in this campaign seems to be paying any attention to the questions they are being asked by the others, even this problem might have been overcome, or otherwise obscured. The *political* difference between overcoming and obscuring a problem is not great, as Wilson knows, and Heath perhaps does not appreciate.

There is a streak of cruelty in Wilson's performance. Many in the press sense it, in that they see Heath as the toyed plaything. Although Heath, it sometimes seems, feels that he is being severely dealt with at his morning press conferences, the fact is otherwise: journalists hold back, fearing to occasion a collapse. Not so with Wilson: when journalists hold back with him, it is because they fear their own deflation.

Wilson has begun to flaunt his own superiority. The performance, justified doubtless on political grounds, is – or has been until the beginning of this week: for I write prematurely, and everything I say must be construed as premature – somewhat gruesome, like bull-fighting, cock-baiting, fish-teasing, hunting, shooting.

'When are you going to let us have a drop of rain for our gardens?' Wilson was asked on Monday. 'I shall have a word or two to say on the subject later in the week,' he replies. He declares, 'It's been a good year for beer.' He says, 'The Tories say they're going to apply general pressure on the wages problem. I don't know who the hell General Pressure is.' He goes outside and there he holds another press conference, this time with small children from the school whose hall he has borrowed. 'Do you think wages should go up for unmarried women?' an eight-year-old asks him. 'I wouldn't give up hope yet, dear,' he replies.

Down the road, Heath says, asked about some Wilson remark on the World Cup, 'I am sure there is no form of triviality to which this man will not descend.' Heath appears profoundly to disapprove of Wilson's frivolity. He keeps asking Wilson, via press conferences and speeches, elaborate questions, then says 'I don't expect in the least any answer from Mr Wilson to my questions.'

Mr Heath says he cannot say whether or not Britain faces economic peril, because he 'hasn't seen the books'. I ask him whether he has asked to see the books: 'Of course not,' he snaps. Someone asks him whether he will reintroduce hereditary peerages. 'That is an improper question. It depends entirely between a Prime Minister and Her Majesty.' 'Isn't that a stuffy answer?' someone asks.

Behind Heath, in his portable Central Office stage set which he takes around the country with him, are a series of concentric circles. Wilson loves these circles. 'They show Heath in the middle,' he says, 'and outside everything is going round in circles. I've also heard it said that they represent a vortex, up into the middle of which Heath will disappear, shortly before polling day.'

It's not fair.

New Statesman, 19 June 1970   *Pamela Hansford*
Johnson

DIRTY STORY

Story of O *by* PAULINE RÉAGE *Olympia Press* 42s

Some months ago, so I was told, a young Frenchman advanced upon an assistant in Liberty's bookshop, crying out gaily, *'Mais, Mademoiselle, où est le porno?'*

Well, here is *le porno*, all right. This stomach turning little book is, and we need make no bones about it, fairly well written, except for the terrible repetitiousness which is, of course, a feature of the *genre*. It comes with an imprimatur in the form of a preface (though it's at the back of the book) by Jean Paulhan, of the French Academy. He sounds rather like a witness in the Chatterley case swearing blue-blind that this was a Puritan work. He talks of the book's 'incredible decency', by which he merely means, I presume, that there are no dirty words in it.

The *Story*, which isn't much of a story, concerns a beautiful Parisienne taken by her lover to a mysterious chateau, equipped with hoods and chains and iron collars, where she is repeatedly violated in every conceivable manner (though the fact that the number of possibilities yielded by the human body are restricted leads to the repetitiousness I have mentioned), chained and beaten and tortured. She appears, however, to love every gorgeous moment of it. 'At this point', writes M. Paulhan, 'some fool is probably going to raise the hue and cry of masochism.' I fail to understand his heat. This is a sado-masochistic work that would have been on the booklist of Brady and Hindley, had it been published in time for them.

I have said that it isn't badly written. This is why it is going to be put out as 'art' and 'literature'. If the writing were shoddy, it would have remained under the counter in the Soho dirty book shops, along with other works as sexually diseased. But if it were as well-written as *À la Recherche* or *Ulysses*, it would be even more pernicious than it is. Above its appeal to the cruelty in us all, its feverish urging upon us of the delights of torture, is a rather spurious and nauseating femininity, which smells like someone's over-scented bathroom. Like *Justine*, it has the reek of patchouli. I believe, but cannot prove, that it may do real harm to those immature, or weak, enough to be taken in by it. Because the publication of this famous piece of smut is a confidence trick. We are being persuaded that it is done in the name of libertarianism.

Now it has to be borne in mind that no one is a total libertarian. If we were to be entirely free from censorship, the Race Relations Act would have to go by the board. *Story of O* may be hailed as the *fine fleure* of our joyful permissiveness. But imagine that a novel in praise of apartheid came into the shops – what an outcry there would be! Whether anyone is dense enough to imagine that I should like to see the Act repealed, I shouldn't. It is an excellent act, except that it has – is bound to have – some silly side-effects. But let us not be mealy-mouthed about libertarianism *in toto*. All that is meant by most libertarians is: 'You shall be utterly free to say what I like to hear you saying!'

Story of O is published because it is frankly pornographic. It takes our liberty to publish, which is precious, to the extreme of licence. If the author had stretched his or her slender talents to writing a book that was as 'clean' as *Eric, or Little by Little*, I much doubt whether it would have seen daylight.

Just as we must not deny our enthusiasms, we must not deny our capacity to be repelled. Boredom means being shocked: this is the charge usually made against anyone who claims to take no pleasure in pornography. But it means no such thing. Boredom may well be the aftermath of shock – it worked that way for me this time. I was shocked, yes: then increasingly bored by what seemed to have become very silly. We absorb shock fast, most of us. But some people don't. The shock effect stimulates every time the cause for it is invoked, and may even lead to the desire for emulation. There is a certain safety in genuine boredom.

This book, with its sticky descriptions of sodomy and fellatio, we might well have been spared. It sickens, and it ought to sicken. If we never react at all to this kind of thing (which I doubt), others do: they are meant to. By our lack of reaction we are put out of danger, and so we can claim only too glibly that this sort of thing does one no harm and *can do others no harm*. This is the toplofty attitude which has run through the whole controversy concerning pornography and violence, and I have elsewhere called it a snob attitude. We are not, of course, yet a sick society; if we were, trains would cease to run for all time and the garbage would accumulate for ever in the streets.

The book is, even at its most ridiculous (the heroine wears a metal chain depending from a ring bored through her genitals), horribly cruel: and cruelty is the worst of all sins. Nothing should be done to encourage it, or to make us accustomed to it: we are all cruel enough in our own ways. *Story of O* is a deliberate incitement to all manner of fancy cruelty, and if we don't know that people *do* do some of these things, then we know nothing.

It is amazing what sort of support this degraded stuff can get. From Mr J. G. Ballard (on the jacket):

Here all kinds of terrors await us, but like a baby taking its mother's milk all pains are assuaged. Touched by the magic of love, everything is transformed. *Story of O* is a deeply moral homily.

Well, if this is a moral homily, God help us. Graham Greene writes: 'A rare thing, a pornographic book well-written and without a trace of obscenity.' What, then, is obscenity? Silly old four-letter words? The mind boggles.

Story of O is written to provoke the familiar visceral response; and here, for the most part, till we see through the trick, it tends to succeed. Can anyone read of torture – a reality in our own day and in some countries – without such a response? This fantasy (it is, of course, a sickly-sweet fetichistic fantasy) deliberately attempts to awaken it. We should none of us be frightened not to be 'with it' if we really find this work pretty appalling. Among other human rights is the right to be appalled, and say so.

Spectator, 27 June 1970   *Martin Seymour-Smith*

GOATS AND MONKEYS

Story of O *by* PAULINE RÉAGE, translated from the French, *Olympia Press* 42s

Histoire d'O first appeared in France in 1954, with a preface by the academician Jean Paulhan. Paulhan, now eighty-six, has had an odd and off-beat career as a writer and critic: he published a volume of Malagasy poetry (1913), and several books of paradoxical short stories (the first in 1915) that anticipated many later modes and procedures, including surrealism. He has studied the twentieth century as an age of terror, and probed the significance of words as acutely as any critic. He is a pioneer figure who may in some ways be compared to Gaston Bachelard – although the range of his inquiries is much more limited and his inclination to erect theories much less intense.

People jumped to the conclusion that Paulhan himself had written the book, but he always insisted that 'Pauline Réage' hid the identity of a woman living in provincial France. Opinion differs about the truth of this; but few now attribute the book to Paulhan. 'Pauline Réage' herself cropped up only once more: as the author of a preface to another pseudonymous erotic novel, 'Jean de Berg's' *L'Image* (1956) – this could, just possibly, be by the same author, although it seems unlikely.

Story of O was published in America in 1966, translated by Sabine D'Estrée. This anonymous Olympia Press version, less colloquial, conveys the deadpan elegance of the French more effectively; Paulhan's excellent preface is reprinted as an epilogue.

Story of O is a highly literary and imaginative work, the brilliance of whose style leaves one in no doubt whatever of the author's genius or of his (or her) ultimately extra-pornographic intentions. It is a profoundly disturbing book, as well as a black *tour de force*. One may have a measure of sympathy with the indignation it arouses: it is, I think, difficult for an uncritical or ill-informed reader to see it as anything but pornographic. For the evidence is that it is sexually arousing (not that there is any harm in this) to many men and women; and its framework is certainly pornographic. Its *genre* was invented by de Sade; its main male character, O's proprietor, the Englishman Sir Stephen, is modelled on the English aristocratic-heroes of countless French nineteenth-century pornotopias. Furthermore, apart from a few astonishingly acute passages of psychological analysis of O's feelings, the whole novel is sexually fantastic in exactly the manner of pornography. None of this could possibly happen.

But *Story of O*, pornography as it is, disturbing – even distressing – as it is, nevertheless transcends its *genre*. The quality of its text justifies its being taken seriously as literature – not simply as material of sociological and psychological interest. *Story of O* is *about* pornography: about fantasy. Its heroine's name, besides its obvious sexual implications, represents both emptiness and fulness. The novel itself might be said to describe the anguish with which the hard and delineated circumference of self wishes to inhabit, vanish into, the vacuity of fear, submission, death.

The Kronhausens, in their surely too perfunctory reference to this book in *Pornography and the Law*, find it interesting because of its 'preoccupation with clothes as psychological sex stimuli' and its 'theme of breaking the woman from her sexual jealousy towards the lover'. They miss the point. What they call the 'clothes fetishism' is, in my view, the clue to the author's feminine identity: the attitude towards clothes displayed is that of a woman, not a man – although O's quest is always to discover her proprietor's taste and to attempt to satisfy it. As for the theme of sexual jealousy; this is merely incidental. This story amounts to an examination of the connection between romantic love and death.

O is not, I believe, the invention of male fantasy. On the contrary, she fantasises men as her masters; by her frantic and voluntary submission to them, by her willingness to be trained by them, and finally to die for them, she actually trains them to destroy her – to turn her into an object. At the end, naked, depilated, hideously mutilated, marked with the whip, led on a chain, exhibited on a terrace, she wears an owl-mask: the writer has achieved, by the efforts of her own fantasy – for this is fantasy, it is deliberately not real, deliberately only words – the wisdom of selflessness, of death. She has both defeated her masters, by leaving them no further ways of humiliating or mastering her, and discovered herself.

Haunting this book, like the 'strong fanatical wind' that Paulhan rightly says blows though it, is the conviction that human sexuality is demonic, extreme, terrible. The mechanics of its masochism seem sometimes to suggest that O's whole submissive project is a gigantic metaphor for the bearing of a child. But the novel itself never for a moment allows that O's love can be anything but fantasy-directed. Her ordeal, 'incredibly decent' (as Paulhan calls it), is essentially a saintly ascent, through torture, to death. She frees herself by embracing absolute degradation. The inevitable corollary is that suffering is there, whatever she (and we) will do. It is not as cosy a message as that offered either by the old Christian ascetics or the new, atheistical pop-clergy; but it has the nobility of an 'incredible decency'. If a love not based in fantasy is accessible to us, we nevertheless need to understand the nature of one that is.

IN OPPOSITION

New Statesman, 26 June 1970   *Tom Baistow*
FLEET STREET SKINHEADS

There are a score of conflicting theories about the reasons for Labour's defeat, but there can be no doubt about the desperate way the right-wing papers put the boot in when it looked as if Wilson had won. For a couple of weeks *The Times, Telegraph, Mail, Express* and *Sketch* exploited every scrap of Labour-knocking 'news' with a single-minded irresponsibility that increased in direct ratio to Labour's rising lead in their polls and culminated in a concerted howl of horror at the fast-approaching economic disaster which, according to their predictions, should be engulfing us any minute.

Yet today (with one curious exception I'll come back to later) economic gloom has disappeared from front pages to make way for a panglossian build-up of Mr Heath and his new-style oldies. What happened to the crisis-round-the-corner, the plunge towards devaluation? In case you missed the miraculous change-round in the situation, let me cite the word of that distinguished observer, Mr David Wood, political editor of *The Times*, which banged the disaster drum with such Canadian vigour. Writing last Saturday, the day after the result, he let the cat out of Mr Rees-Mogg's carpet-bag halfway through a splash about the new government's opening manoeuvres. 'The tax changes will need time,' reported Mr Wood, 'and, *short of a sudden crisis that nobody expects*, an emergency budget is extremely unlikely.' The outraged italics are mine.

It would take a large book to document and analyse the papers' shameless management of the news to fit the Tory need for a prices/devaluation crisis, but a couple of typical examples of the way economic and law-and-order issues were handled make it painfully clear how millions of voters – or, probably more important, non-voters – were conditioned by the majority of the national press. The trade figures, coming two days before polling day, were of course a gift to the Right. But not good enough for the *Mail*, which proceeded to put the Tory Central Office propagandists to shame. Under a banner that screamed: '18s for your £ by 1971' it declared: 'The worst of all possible economic worlds, with stagnation and inflation. This is the picture of Britain's economic situation painted by the Treasury yesterday. Shop prices rose by 9d in the £ in the first four months of this year ... the first four months' experience suggests inflation at the horrifying rate of more than 10 per cent. This means that the pound on New Year's Day would be worth 18s by next Christmas.' Would it? The very next paragraph went on to state quite unabashedly that *'The Treasury expects the rate of increase in shop prices to slow down this summer*, but there's no sign of it yet.' (My italics.) The sheer audacity of the bold headline must have fooled many a reader.

At least one must give the *Mail* credit for tenacity. Last Wednesday, just a week later – seven days is a long time in journalism – its splash cried 'Wilson's Sums All Wrong' and declared that in its *latest* assessment the Treasury gave the lie to his claim that Mr Heath has inherited the strongest economy of any PM. 'Ministers,' it announced solemnly, 'find themselves landed with that awful combination – stagnation and inflation.' Surprise, Surprise! Why, you might wonder, is that old familiar bogey stagnation/inflation supposed to be *news* when this was allegedly the picture the Treasury was painting a week before? One had to read on and between the lines to find the answer: 'The Treasury will probably argue against rapid growth, tax cuts and borrowing controls because they might fuel inflation, suck in imports and gobble up our balance of payments surplus.' Exactly. As Mr Jenkins pointed out so often. In other words, that never-never land of tax-slashing and hands-off-the-handlebars free enterprise which Mr Heath promised to pay the bearers of Tory party cards on demand is going to be indefinitely deferred.

So much for the economic sleight of hand. Remember the law-and-order campaign, the bring-back-hanging demands, the 'biggest-ever crime wave' scare handed to the press on a plate by the man Mr Heath has chosen as his Lord Chancellor, Mr Quintin Hogg? True, the Tories dropped it in favour of rising prices when the cancellation of the South African cricket tour dashed their hopes of demo punch-ups, but one might have hoped, without being too naive, that a remarkable drop in the number of murders in 1969 – down 23, to 125 – would have been spared the election treatment. The *Telegraph*, while finding room on page one for more attractive statistics, 'Strikes up 65 per cent', put the murder figures on page 2; it had the grace, however, to point out that the number which would have qualified as capital offences under the 1957 Act also dropped by four to 38. *The Times* gave a brief summary at the foot of an inside page and the others, so far as I could see, just ignored it.

We can add one murder to the 1970 figures: editorial fairness, done in by Fleet Street's skinheads.

New Statesman, 9 October 1970   *Paul Johnson*
SHADOW AND SPECTRE AT NUMBER 10

The new Prime Minister looks considerably more relaxed, thank
goodness, than the old Leader of the Opposition. He is even, in his
curious way, enjoying himself. The nightmare of last week's Labour
party conference – that Labour, thanks to Messrs Jones and Scanlon,
may get itself so hopelessly identified with the wages free-for-all as to
expose itself to a disastrous snap election on the trade union issue –
seems a delightful fantasy to Ted Heath. If that were his plan, he laughs,
then he wouldn't be telling anyone about it, would he? But seriously
(end of smile), that was not at all the way he thought about politics; by
no means; it might, of course, be the approach of a certain other person.

Evidently the spectre of Harold Wilson often flits across the
Premier's mind. Discussing his plans, there are frequent asides about
'my predecessor', usually in tones of pity and condescension, not
wholly unmixed with awe; so Gladstone, newly returned to Number 10,
might have descanted on the evils of Beaconsfieldism, swinging the
while an imaginary purifying censer. The obsession is hardly surprising.
As party leader, Heath was first told to be as like Wilson as possible;
then the opposite. The second instruction was more congenial. But in
one way or another, Wilson still seems to colour everything Heath does.
His first three months in office only make sense on the assumption that
he is consciously trying to act in as un-Wilsonian a manner as possible.
He even plans his day, he says, to allow plenty of time for deep
cogitation; no hand-to-mouth, instant-reaction politics for him. You'd
think he was still Shadow Prime Minister, as in a sense he is. How he
must, indeed does, hate 'the little man'; but the little man still haunts him
across the cabinet table, follows him up the stairs to the flat, perches
jauntily on his pillow at night. Not all the Omo and Ajax in the
supermarket can quite efface that pervasive presence – yet.

And, after all, the two men have something very important in
common: they are dedicated careerists in the most exacting of trades.
When the Admissions Tutor at Balliol asked Edward Heath what he
intended to be in life, the answer was crisp: 'A professional politician.'
There was a perceptible raising of Balliol eyebrows. That very secular
establishment is familiar with ambition – may indeed encourage it. But
not even Balliol had heard the answer put in quite such terms.
Moreover, it was accurate. Politics – and Conservative politics – have

been Heath's aim since his first recorded utterance at grammar school.
No one, not even Harold Wilson, has striven more consistently and
energetically to acquire the skills of the parliamentary politician than
Heath. True, for an aspiring Tory, certain disadvantages of
background had to be overcome, though they were not so formidable as
the myth would now have us believe. Heath can trace his family back to
1739; very few Englishmen can do as much. His father did well enough
to maintain himself, during the Great Depression, as an independent
builder: the perfect setting, indeed, for a self-made Tory son. But
caution, self-discipline, enormous concentration and industry were
needed; above all, no mistakes. 'Teddy always used to prefer people
older than himself,' says his father.

   In the political hot house of pre-war Oxford, Heath struck a nicely-
judged posture, combining Tory orthodoxy with a strong dash of anti-
Appeasement. He was, says Harold Macmillan, 'conspicuous for his
skill and enthusiasm' in the famous 1938 Oxford by-election,
campaigning for A. D. Lindsay against the official Tory, Quintin Hogg,
under the slogan 'A Vote for Hogg is a Vote for Hitler'. (The fact is not
forgotten in a certain quarter; the day Heath was elected party leader,
Hogg was heard to remark, with grim joviality: 'Now we must fasten
our seatbelts.') But no doubt was allowed to be cast on Heath's
fundamental Tory allegiance. He was a highly efficient boss of the
University Conservative Club, a Tory President of the Union and, to
cap everything, President of the Balliol JCR. 'A thoroughly successful,
well-established Balliol figure,' says his junior contemporary, Roy
Jenkins, adding: 'More self-confident than he is now.' 'There was a solid
virtue and steadiness about him,' intones Lord Fulton, 'industry applied
to the right points, sensible and self-controlled use of his time.' Another
Balliol figure, Hugh Fraser, puts it a bit differently: 'Very competent,
but there was no great ebullience of youth.' To quote Cousin Jasper in
Brideshead Revisited, Heath represented 'the stiffer element in college'.

   Heath's biographer calls his war record 'conventionally distinguished'. 'Never put a foot wrong,' says one witness; and another:
'Meticulously correct in conduct and behaviour.' A gunner, Heath
spent most of the war doing anti-aircraft in Britain, but there was just
time for a good campaign in Germany and the rank of lieutenant-
colonel. More important, there was follow-up afterwards. Wartime
ranks are soon forgotten or, if consciously retained, merely irritate.
Heath stayed on as a territorial, became a colonel in the Honourable
Artillery Company, and a Master Gunner of the Tower of London.
These things count for a good deal at all levels in the Tory party.

   He chose his occupation carefully, too. As part of his professional politician's equipment, he decided to 'see the civil service from the inside', took the Administrative Class exam, passed out top of the list, and spent a profitable two years at Civil Aviation, under the exacting (but impressed) Peter Masefield. He left his mark there, but cheerfully threw up his job, as regulations demanded, when he was adopted as Tory candidate for Bexley in 1947. The best the University Appointments Board could do for him, in the meantime, was the news-editorship of the *Church Times*. It was uncongenial work; he did it competently and no more. He did not mix much with the staff (though he took the proprietor's son to lunch with the Honourable Company); the episode is not mentioned in his *Who's Who* entry; and he escaped, as soon as occasion offered, to the more appropriate and useful world of merchant banking.

Bexley returned Heath to Parliament, after an anxious recount, in 1950. In the House, he was obviously Whip material, and a Whip he promptly became. Except for two or three months, Heath has never sat on the back benches. First as Assistant, then Deputy, then (1955–9) Chief Whip, his first decade in Parliament was exclusively confined to discipline and organisation. He had no opportunity to cut a parliamentary figure, little chance indeed to speak at all. He still suffers from the handicap of these silent years, and from the habits then formed: only an ex-Chief Whip could have handled Enoch Powell quite so fiercely. On the other hand his job enabled him to acquire a unique knowledge of his colleagues in Parliament; he was generous with his time in the constituencies, cultivating the acquaintance, if not exactly the friendship, of innumerable modest but collectively influential functionaries. No Tory leader since Chamberlain has possessed anything like Heath's grasp of the party machine – at all its levels. Moreover, he was a very effective Chief Whip; he did not relish the Suez business, but he held the party together during those desperate days and, next to Macmillan himself, he was the strategist of the Tory revival and the 1959 triumph; all this without making an enemy. Many Tories still remember his work as Whip with gratitude; some claim that, had he kept the office, the errors of Macmillan's decline would have been avoided.

At any rate, these services were his chief executive claim to the leadership when the time came. For, as a minister, Heath was not a success by the test that matters. His spell at Labour was brief and uneventful. As Lord Privy Seal he handled the Common Market negotiations, and there is no doubt that he wielded plenary powers in Brussels. His periodic reports to Tory backbenchers on the talks impressed by their lucidity, detail and authority. But it became apparent that the project had been misconceived from the start – by Heath no less than Macmillan. There were plenty, too, who argued that his tactics in Brussels – his obstinacy in delaying concessions which were inevitable – had contributed to the debacle. He denies this; he says that on the Friday before De Gaulle's press conference, at a tête-à-tête dinner with Couve de Murville, Couve conceded that Britain was in; evidently neither he nor Pompidou knew what De Gaulle was about to do. Be this as it may, the policy was a failure.

His only other major venture as a minister was, technically, a triumph; as President of the Board of Trade he fought through the abolition of retail price maintenance against resolute opposition in the cabinet, on the back benches and in the constituencies. He aroused a good deal of resentment, and for the first time made enemies. Once the Bill became law, the excitement quickly subsided, and is now forgotten. It was soon seen that no great harm had been done; no great good, either. The whole episode was a waste of the party's emotional energy, at a time when it was badly needed.

What saved his career was, ironically, the elevation of Home to the premiership. The idea that Tories take naturally to upper-crust leaders is a myth. A disreputable upstart like Disraeli could never have led the Whigs, or the Liberals, and least of all Labour. There is, among the more active Tories, a recurrent vein of resentment against aristocratic rule. Criticism of the 'Hotel Cecil' led to 'Balfour Must Go'. In 1912 the Tories preferred a first-generation Canadian-Scottish adventurer, Bonar Law, to Austen Chamberlain, an industrial aristocrat, and Walter Long, spokesman of the landed interest. Curzon lost the leadership not so much because he was a peer, but because he behaved like one. The very idea that Home had been put in by 'the magic circle' – for which there was no less an authority than Iain Macleod – made it certain that his tenure would be challenged and (unless crowned by improbable success) brief. It was also certain that his successor would benefit from his very different origins.

Now all this posed a problem for Heath. He had industriously pursued his career with the object of overcoming what were felt to be social handicaps; now it suddenly became politic to emphasise them. He had endeavoured to cast himself in the Macmillan-Eden mould: Balliol, army service, territorial gold-braid, merchant banking, dress, voice, gestures, even the well-worn clichés. His efforts had not been wholly successful; the vowel-sounds, surprisingly in a musician, remained obstinate. But on the whole he had done a good job. Now, with his chances really serious, a certain anxious reconstruction of the image had to be undertaken at short notice.

The task was complicated by the Wilson factor; Wilson had made parliamentary mincemeat of the Fourteenth Earl. What was needed, then, was a Tory leader not only of comparable origins but of comparable acerbity. So there was born abrasive Ted (he had ceased to be 'Teddy', except to his family). The evidence that Ted was in fact abrasive, or able to slug it out with Wilson on the floor of the House, was non-existent; but in the excitement which followed Home's abrupt departure, it was somehow taken for granted. The idea was put about that here was a decent, honourable chap who nevertheless, when the party required, could behave in a thoroughly ungentlemanly manner: just what the doctor ordered. Of course professionalism helped. Ted's campaign was run on a no-chances-taken basis by Peter Walker. By comparison, Maudling's efforts, such as they were, looked amateurish. The issue was determined when Macleod stood down, thus allowing precious votes to switch to Heath. The party had come a long way from the days when 'too clever by half' was damaging.

Heath thus became leader as a Tory Harold Wilson. The illusion was general: Tories as diverse as Home, Macleod, Whitelaw, Barber, Joseph and Boyle (it is believed) voted for him. But it was soon dispelled. Wilson made mincemeat of Heath, too; only with more relish; and Heath got far less sympathy – it was as though he had, poor man, been found out on a false prospectus. Far from shining in the Commons, he sent the Tories back to school, in endless committees and sub-committees, which churned out mountains of material that no one (save himself) read. Gruesome names like Sundridge Park and Selsdon Park were branded on reluctant Tory breasts. Abrasive Ted could not fill the House; but he could empty drawing-rooms as he stood, shoulders heaving with anxious cordiality, spreading ever widening ripples of unease and silence. There were mutterings, even wistful sighs for the return of the Earl.

But it all came out right in the end. As Wilsonism became devalued, so the need to match it disappeared. On the contrary: the requirement was now for someone who looked as unlike Wilson as possible. Here Heath came much closer to fitting the bill. No generous imagination could make him the Rupert of Debate; but a convincing case could be made that he was responsible, honest, trustworthy, industrious, unflashy, worthy and dull. Thus the image-makers came back to square one. Whether it did the trick in June we shall never really know. Certainly there was no evident confidence in Heath Mark Three until the very second the first result came in. At a party for personal staff afterwards, he had some brief words of gratitude for those who stood by him, as he put it, 'in the dark days' – a most uncharacteristic admission.

As Premier, he faces a sea of troubles, some of his own making. He over-prepared himself for office, and is thus lumbered with commitments beyond reason – some contracted in the panic weeks before polling day when he thought he was going to lose. A great many people, for instance, have the clearest possible recollection that he promised, without apparent qualification, to reduce prices. He inherits a chronically weak economy and a confusion of political aims among both the major parties, induced by the need to win elections. Thus, in 1963–4 the Tories found themselves, against all their principles, launching an enormous programme of state expenditure; equally, in 1969–70, Labour in desperation virtually abandoned any attempt to control the economy, and especially wages and prices.

Whether Heath, whose own electoral position is far from secure, can break out of this vicious pattern, and if so on what basis, remains to be seen. No clear set of beliefs emerges from anything he has written, said or done, other than a low-keyed assumption that the free-enterprise world is the oyster of the lower-middle classes; he mutters about 'incentives' and so forth; perhaps his *credo* can best be put as: 'Suburban man can save himself by his exertions, and Britain by his example.' He is unlikely to get much inspiration from his colleagues, some of whom are tired relics from the Macmillan era, others prematurely flyblown. That is really not his fault. As Lloyd George put it in a secret memorandum to Asquith, advocating a coalition in 1910: 'No party commands the services of more than half-a-dozen first-rate men and it has to depend for the filling up of all the other posts in the government on the services of men of second- and even third-rate capacity.' 'Half-a-dozen' seems generous in Heath's case; and the loss of Macleod – the best debater and the only powerful romantic force in the government – was a devastating blow, perhaps more serious than he yet knows.

The new Premier has now had ample time to survey the political horizons. At home, he does not share the current obsession with incomes policy. The Tories, he says, tried it on a voluntary basis; Labour brought in compulsion; neither worked. He prefers to talk in terms of a wider economic policy, controlled by action on the public sector, government spending, credit and taxation, which together will create a framework for stability, with wages finding their natural level. It is not very convincing. Abroad, he sees three areas of new flexibility: East–West relations in Europe, thanks to Brandt's initiative; the Middle East, thanks to the disappearance of Nasser; and South East Asia, thanks to Nixon's evident (to Heath) determination to disengage in Vietnam. Africa, he thinks, is a more rigid field than before, thanks to 'my predecessor'. He was disturbed to find, on returning to office, how sharply Britain's influence had declined in the meantime, again thanks to you-know-who; but a return to the East of Suez policy should put that right; it was not even going to be expensive; surprisingly cheap, in fact. Well, we shall see.

We shall also see how far he is prepared to risk his future to achieve the object he desires above all else in politics: entry into Europe. He insists that he is not a 'get-in-first-and-then-reform-from-within' Marketeer; he knows too much about the small print of the Rome Treaty for such illusions. If the price is too high, he says, it could bankrupt us; and there is disconcerting evidence that the price is likely to be higher than in the early Sixties, for terms then agreed are now being reopened on French insistence. On the other hand, the vital importance he attaches to securing entry becomes apparent once he gives his view of the alternatives; there are, he says, no alternatives. We will just have to carry on as we are. The impression he leaves is that, short of complete capitulation, he will get a document for Parliament to ratify; and that Parliament will do as it is bid.

In short, Heath is likely to prove a 'strong' Prime Minister. He is a solitary and politically friendless man – excellent qualifications for the post. He has given no hostages, owes precious few debts. His self-confidence has been enormously enhanced by triumphantly surviving the truly horrible ordeal of the last few years. Labour, and indeed his own followers, have already thrown the book at him; and he is still there. Everything in his career suggests that he is massively determined when his mind is made up. He is now respected; he will soon be very much feared, and not only on his side of the House. His resolution is such that one can see him (like Peel, whom he so much resembles) risking all in pursuit of a monumental policy; in this sense, Hogg's 'fasten your seatbelts' could be apt. He still seems, for instance, determined to pursue his idea of an Anglo-French nuclear force, as part of his overall European policy. But he will concentrate his energies, in the first instance, on making his domestic position unassailable, from without and within.

Spectator, 21 November 1970　　　　　*Peter Paterson*
MR BENN AND THE REFERENDUM

If Mr Anthony Wedgwood Benn – the thinking man's politician – seeks a text for his argument that Britain's signature to the Treaty of Rome should be decided not by a parliamentary vote but by a national referendum, he will find it in Tom Payne's *Rights of Man*, appropriately enough in the section headed, 'Ways and Means of improving the condition of Europe, interspersed with Miscellaneous Observations'.

'Rebellion,' stated Mr Payne [*sic*], 'consists in forcibly opposing the general will of a nation, whether by a party or by a government. There ought, therefore, to be in every nation a method of occasionally ascertaining the state of public opinion with respect to government.' Now, it may be argued that the old revolutionary was not talking about referenda, and certainly not what people today would call opinion poll government. But nor was he talking about occasionally elected Parliaments, for he went on to give a little pat on the back to the French monarchical system of the States-General. One may be permitted to assume that confronted by the tendency of modern British political parties to stand for election on the broadest possible platform, Tom Payne would have been in favour of a referendum to decide so historic and momentous a change of course as Britain's surrender of national sovereignty to the European Economic (and Political) Community.

As one of the successors, as an MP for Bristol, of Edmund Burke, Mr Benn might have been expected to take a far more traditionalist line on the duty of an MP towards his constituents. The Burke dictum, that an MP owes his constituents not only his industry but his judgement 'and he betrays instead of serving you if he sacrifices it to your opinion . . .' will no doubt be much quoted against Mr Benn, and invoked by pro-Market MPs in the great battle which is to come. But if we are playing historical games for a moment, we may also question whether Burke would stick to his own principle if he interpreted membership of the Market as jeopardising the terms of the Revolution of 1688. So let's claim, before anyone else does, that Payne and Burke as well as Benn would have been for a referendum.

That, unfortunately, is probably not sufficient to recommend it to Mr Heath or Mr Rippon, or even to Mr Harold Wilson, though if the latter had recovered fully from his electoral reverse he might have been expected to see the glittering opportunity that a referendum on this issue could present him with, without his having particularly to bother changing his stated policy towards Market entry. That opportunity lies in the proposition that the present Government would not be strong enough to survive an adverse vote on a referendum, and would almost inevitably be defeated in the general election that would follow.

Mr Benn is not the kind of politician who would argue for the referendum on such grounds, or with such thoughts lurking in his mind. More than any of his contemporaries on either side of the House, Mr

Benn brings an independent and unorthodox attitude to political problems. If he is worried about pollution, for example, or the remoteness of government, or the lack of accountability of the technologists, he thinks pretty carefully before delivering his views, and when he does so he usually has something refreshing and interesting to say. This does not make him a political Fauntleroy, and he is probably more capable than most other politicians of putting his foot in it, often in the most embarrassing way at the most embarrassing moment. But when he is being serious, there is no more serious man in politics.

Unfortunately, Mr Benn's career has been studded with plenty of examples reflecting both sides of his personality, and such is the nature of politics that his more lighthearted or excitable or partisan contributions have tended to obscure some of the important things he has to say.

The question that his past forces us to ask, therefore, is: are we sure that Mr Benn is being serious on this occasion? There are obviously grounds for the suspicion that he is not. First of all, he is the first professing Marketeer to call for a referendum. Since a referendum, it is assumed by most people, would reject British entry by a very substantial majority, the doubt must arise that Mr Benn remains a Marketeer any longer. If he has indeed changed his views on this question, then his advocacy of a referendum loses its surprise value and he becomes just another anti-Marketeer seizing on any device that will prevent Britain going in.

Another area of doubt concerns Mr Benn's views on participation. Unsophisticated believers in political participation by what are usually, and disparagingly, called the masses have a great belief in everything being decided by a vote, preferably on a show of hands at a public meeting, and a great contempt for Members of Parliament and the parliamentary system. Mr Benn is not unsophisticated, and he combines a genuine belief in wider participation with a respect, even reverence, for the parliamentary process. A national referendum on the Market, it could and very likely will be argued, is a blasphemy against Parliament. Is he really being serious when he argues for it?

Again, we all recall Mr Benn as Labour's Minister of Technology full of whizz kid boffinry, mad keen on Concorde (at least in public) and sufficiently delighted by the idea of international cooperation that he allowed the French to add the final 'e'. Mr Benn's internationalist brand of socialism, his belief that the power of international corporations can make life intolerable for national governments, his knowledge of the immense amounts of money that must be pooled if Europe is to compete in technology with the United States, all made it understandable that he should veer towards the idea of the European Community. Why then should he now argue for a referendum, a vote that will be decided, according to all the other pro-Marketeers, not on technological considerations, not on the future of Concorde-type projects, not on taming IBM or General Motors, but on the price of groceries? So, does he mean it?

The answer seems to be that Mr Benn is serious, that he does mean it, and that he is pressing for it in spite of, rather than because of, his views on the Market – though it may be doubted whether those views are quite as strong as they once were. But this is an issue on which many people have chopped and changed, and one of the reasons for this is that the issues raised by British entry to or isolation from the Market have never been bound together in one great debate in which all aspects could be argued and a firm decision reached. Information has emerged in dribs and drabs, so that at one moment the case for going in seems overwhelming (this was the position for many MPs during the 1966 economic crisis) and at another (when the White Paper on the effect of entry on food prices and the balance of payments was published) when it seems unthinkable.

Political leadership, with Tories, Labour and Liberals all in favour, has been gravely damaged by anti-Marketeers within, at least, the two major parties. People are naturally confused when they see national figures disagreeing with the party leaders on an issue of such magnitude, and possibly even more alarmed when it is suggested that no final decision can be taken before the full terms of entry are finally negotiated. When that time comes, Mr Benn suggests, a narrow majority of the Cabinet and a narrow majority of the House of Commons could take a decision which would, for good or ill, be quite irreversible. If we assume that he would be part of that majority, it is the first sign of nervousness we have yet seen among that group over the gravity of the responsibility they will bear for the decision and its consequences.

Mr Benn is right to be nervous. But the value of a referendum would surely be greater than merely to make the waverers feel that they are no longer opposing the general will of the nation. It would give the first and only opportunity for the issue to be debated by the British people, uncluttered by all the other considerations that affect the outcome of a general election. And after that process, as any opinion pollster could have told us on 19 June, no one could be certain of the outcome.

New Statesman, 26 March 1971   *Kenneth Allsop*
MR VORSTER'S SHOWPLACE

All of us flash our passes – 50 cent conducted tour tickets – and are directed by the city council receptionist to follow the red arrows pasted in the corridor. We straggle obediently, strangers not yet tucked up in the char-à-banc togetherness to come. There is an elderly American in a General Abrams duckbilled cap (but in peacock paisley) and his wife wimpled with sequined mist-blue gauze, and in our number are a few bearing a blurred British look. Most of the clatter, though, is in Afrikaans: children with parents and a school party of teenagers, oddly frumpish and short-haired, out-of-towners on a visit to Johannesburg. Are they on this Tour of Bantu Townships for education or entertainment?

At first it is primly educational. In the Non-European Affairs Department's lecture room (wall-to-wall carpeting, aerial photographs labelled 'ethnic groupings') we are welcomed by a stony, air hostess smile. The brooch says she is Jen. She is a buxom young woman, with sandy kiss curls, who is not only regulation white but rather doughily pale. She has an even voice which glides across her emotive material with the passionless clarity of a telephone answering service.

'The official term, Bantu, means "the people". It includes different tribes of essentially rural nomads. At the turn of the century, Johannesburg's Bantu population was primarily male, itinerant labourers here to accumulate capital to take back to their villages. Then their womenfolk began coming, and families started to settle, but it was the war which brought disastrous results.'

Her bland vanilla look traverses us unseeingly. 'Booming industry demanded more and more labour. The Bantu streamed in unchecked in their tens of thousands. Shanty towns, built of packing cases, cardboard, tin and mud, flooded over the bare veldt. Disease was rife. Packs of starving dogs roamed the streets. Various unscrupulous people in the slums established power over others. These were indeed cruel conditions.'

As the drama darkens, Jen's tone does not change. At the same stilted lilt she approaches the inspiring climax: the cleansing of the horror.

'In 1951 the Bantu Building Workers Act was passed, and Bantu artisans could be trained to erect houses for themselves. Then in 1956 the late Sir Ernest Oppenheimer, millionaire, mine-owner and philanthropist, appalled at the conditions still existing, prevailed upon his colleagues to put up six million rand – the injection of capital the city had needed. In one year the worst slums were cleared. Soweto had begun. Now, everybody, we will go and see what has been done. Please follow me.'

We troop after Jen out into the sun beating down blindingly on Melrose Street. The coach awaits. We sink into luxiseats, from overhead grilles comes piped music: 'Up, up and aw-aaaay in my beautiful balloon . . .' Into her stick mike Jen says: 'Before we start I wish to introduce your driver, William.' The driver swivels, smiling. 'Hi, Bill!' calls out the forage-capped American. Friendly greetings; shining sun; holiday music; Palm Beach shirts. There is the feeling of a fun outing, destination Disneyland – or an enclosure of some sort, named South Western Townships, or Soweto for short.

The coach squeezes through the narrow back streets and out on to glary cement highways; between enormous khaki flat-topped ziggurats, gold-mine spoil; through patchy parkland feathery with bluegums, where egrets skim across thin grass. The cordon sanitaire. Ten miles out we reach a sign, BANTU RESETTLEMENT BOARD, the portcullis of the white man's fortress, and we turn into blackland.

The scenery doesn't change again for the next two hours: oceans of asbestos-roofed flimsy brick huts. They brim in the huge shallow valley, crest it, and then fill the next, and the one after that, and the one beyond, and others on both sides for 25 square miles. It is an astonishing vista, a munificence of bleakness, a prodigality of shoddy ugliness for which one's mind races to find parallels. Moscow's suburbs? The council estates outside Glasgow? Our North Country mill workers' 19th-century tenements? All have a bearing; but put together they can't measure up to this systematised scale of engineered desolation and dinginess.

Jen points to the virtues of size. 'Here is a men's hostel which houses 5,000 single men' – processions of asbestos roofs, frilled with barbed wire. 'This is the non-European general hospital. It will cover 133 acres when completed, the biggest in the world. And here is Orlando power station. Eighty-five per cent of the streets have electricity. An interesting statistic is that many inhabitants with electricity still prefer cooking by the traditional methods of wood or coal.'

So are the anthropological points made, casually but cogently, as our coach cruises on through the sullenly drab maze. Children playing on corner patches of hard bare earth beam and chirrup and wave. We wave back, encouragingly or uneasily according to inner stirrings. Mile after mile of die-stamp hutments until a chill melancholy permeates the coach, affecting everyone, it seems, except Jen and her mechanical brightness: 'We plant two fruit trees for every house. Generally an apricot tree and a peach tree are chosen.'

'Now here' – Jen's words are spaced like the captions in a child's picture book – 'is one little house, that one with the palm tree, which will do well in the gardening competition, I think. And on the left is a lovely little house, with a garden terraced right down to the street. There is the tenant. He is very proud of his garden. He is clipping the lawn . . .'

The way the tour is taking us, Soweto is getting better and better – why, narrow your eyes and you might be in Hampstead Garden Suburb. 'This house has 18 rooms and three bathrooms, cost 85,000 rand, and is owned by one of Soweto's millionaires . . .' But we have also passed ramshackle rows of shops: Fish and Chips, Kwa Mlalal Self Help Cash Store, the Self Helping Hand Funeral Parlour and Mortuary. Great emphasis is placed upon self help and standing on your own two feet, stony though the ground is. Hoardings stuck on waste lots advertise 'Karroo Complexion Cream'; 'Artra Lightens Your Skin'; 'Things Go Better With Big, Big Coke'. One placard, 40 feet high, says LIFE IS GREAT; it shows a pack of 'Life' king-size filters.

We stop before the chic angularity of the Urban Bantu Council building. One of the staff, a middle-aged black trustee* in shirt and tie, addresses us. He recites the constitutional facts. Questions are invited.

Why are the townships divided ethnically? Government policy. What happens to a woman who is deserted or widowed? She must leave the house. Where does she go? Perhaps she will find lodgings. How many people may live in one house? Two families. How many rooms in the house? Two rooms. How does a worker qualify for a house? By having lived in the area 15 years or by having worked for one employer for 10. How long does it take to get a house then? Depends how many are vacated and how many the government has built. How many were built last year? Four hundred and six. How many people on the waiting list? Eleven thousand. So how long will it take to house that 11,000? An uncomfortable pause. He smiles and shrugs. 'I don't know.' Jen decides that question time has gone on long enough. She leads her herd back aboard. We drive out of the compound, toward the raw sawn-off skyscrapers of Johannesburg.

Jen's commentary has missed some details. How many people do live in Soweto, doubled-up and sub-tenanted? The official figure is 550,000. The Africans, nearer to actuality, say 800,000, making Soweto bigger than Durban. Were all those nasty 'unscrupulous

* Trusty? – K.A.

people' – the gangsters and *tsotsi* hoodlums dismantled along with the shanty towns? Available crime figures don't indicate so: on a holiday weekend, when there's time for concentrated drinking, up to 100 citizens die violent deaths in Soweto.

One returns to the sumptuous white suburbia on the jacaranda-smothered northern heights of Johannesburg wondering why the government puts on this bizarre and seedy tourist attraction. One explanation is that apartheid at its most absurd and gross is now embattled not only outside the republic but within, by the widespread 'enlightened' pressure to increase productive and economic efficiency by admitting blacks to skilled, labour-starved trades. So the government has decided to be 'frank' and to let visitors see for themselves, within certain guidelines, of course. Another explanation, macabrely risible at first thought, but which stands up to scrutiny, is that the authorities are genuinely proud of what organisation has achieved.

A booklet entitled *Soweto: A City Within a City* bestows the densest miasma of schizophrenia. Laid out with gorgeous snaps of gay smiling blacks amid sunshine and blossom, it combines a winsome sentimentality and fantasy so 'bleached' in the American racial sense – that one can only believe that it is believed. 'Soweto is not ideal, as the housing is often monotonous, and facilities sometimes few', the booklet concedes artlessly, and then: 'A new spirit is abroad. . . .' Among the photographs illustrating the high standard of life and leisure for the fortunate Sowetoians is one of a black niblick-swinger, one showing three black pals lounging beside a tree-framed lake (caption: 'Taking a breather'), and one showing a ballroom competition, black man in tails, black girl in organdie, just like 'Come Dancing' anywhere in the civilised world.

I had a recollection of the wounded nobility of a Nuremberg defendant rhapsodising about how well run and hygienic Belsen had been before typhoid had so unhappily broken out.

Spectator, 6 March 1971   *J. Enoch Powell*
THE MORALITY OF PROFIT

'Profit has become a dirty word'; or, 'profit ought not to be a dirty word'; or, 'socialism has made profit a dirty word'. These, and statements like them, are a commonplace of Conservative platforms and of business association dinners. The speakers refute, to their own satisfaction and the satisfaction of their audiences, the imputation of 'dirtiness' about profit. Yet the connotation clings. Perhaps there have been periods and places where profit enjoyed a good repute with the public and a good conscience with those who lived by it; but they are not easy to come by or to document. The uneasy suspicion arises that the propensity to regard profit as 'dirty', so far from being a temporary aberration, which must yield to reasoned argument, is normal, deep-seated and pervasive. Maybe the paradox of capitalist societies which disapprove of capitalism is one of those paradoxes of human nature which can't be cured and must be endured.

The reflection is prompted by a little book* in which Professor Acton defends the market, price and profit, and the rest of the mechanism of capitalism against the charge of being immoral, or morally inferior, and in particular selfish. He has it quite easy. It is not difficult to argue – to demonstrate, even – that the alternative to the market and the capitalist process is necessarily inimical to freedom of thought and action, because centralised judgement and compulsion are the only substitutes for the impersonal and spontaneous working of the market. Since all good things are scarce, the elimination of competition and the search for equality means that somebody must apportion and enforce: 'to press for universal distributive justice is to press for a universal authority'. Moreover, the businessman and the capitalist is expected to obey – and indeed must obey, if he is to perform his social function properly – the moralities appropriate to his capacity as businessman or capitalist, and these do not excuse or debar him from observing the rest of the moral code in his other capacities.

Yet the fact remains that the unpopularity of profit has proved throughout the ages impervious to these and similar arguments. Why?

An attractive case, superficially, can be made out that this is the product of class antagonism and prejudice. The nobleman, the landowner, and the warrior despise the very different virtues of the merchant or manufacturer, and may be heard doing so from Plato's *Republic* to Disraeli's *Coningsby*. Other classes besides these may be naturally antagonistic to the capitalist. The priesthood of any religion, and above all of the world-denying religions, finds itself making assertions and inculcating doctrines not reconcilable with the world where capitalism, price and profit are at home. The injunctions to 'sell all thou hast and follow me' and to 'take no care for the morrow' or the observation that 'the love of money is the root of all evil' do not sit comfortably with the business of the market-place, and were not intended to do so. It is not therefore surprising that capitalism, under

* *The Morals of Markets: An Ethical Exploration* by H. B. Acton. Longman (£1.75).

the guise of 'usury', was condemned alike by the Jewish law and the medieval Church, and that Christianity has ever been found among the critics rather than the apologists of the market economy. Then, it has often been pointed out that the professional and academic classes have their own reasons for being contemptuous or hostile towards the market and its works. The type of personality which tends to be attracted into the professions is one that places a relatively high valuation not only on financial security but on the non-monetary rewards of any course of action or way of life. This is the antithesis of the entrepreneurial character, which is attracted by a combination of risk with preponderantly monetary satisfaction and is habituated to measuring off values in monetary terms. Both the professional man and the academic moreover are likely to be repelled by the automatic and spontaneous functioning of the market: accustomed in their own sphere to the supremacy of the intellect, they are hard to persuade that a planned economy would not be superior to a 'blind' market economy, and exhibit towards the businessman the natural arrogance of the man of thought to the man of action. There is thus a good, sound, built-in reason why universities and places where they teach or research should be preponderantly 'left'.

Yet when all this has been said, it is not enough. It does not explain why far and wide beyond all these classes there is a rooted moral prejudice against the basic workings of capitalism. People generally who live and work in a capitalist society and know no other are prone to rail against profit and to view the price mechanism with distaste. The very entrepreneur himself, if you take him in a leisure hour or unguarded moment, is more likely than not to exhibit, not so much an ignorance (though that is common), but a positive dislike of the principles of capitalism by which he lives, and will probably take the opportunity to explain that he is guided, or wishes he could be guided, by rules of a higher morality than those of the market-place. There is a secret shame about being an entrepreneur which there is not about being an artisan or an artist, a lawyer or even a legislator.

We are thus presented with the paradox of an economy, a society, even a civilisation, where the processess by which it exists and flourishes meet with more disapproval than approval when they are consciously exposed and analysed. It is as if a creature whose evolution had provided it with lungs were secretly ashamed of breathing, or with fins, of swimming. There *is* a paradox here; but, I ask again, is it not a paradox common, perhaps universal? If it is, then we cannot close our minds to the further suspicion that it may perhaps therefore have a necessary and salutary function. In terms: is there an evolutionary law that favours organisms and societies in which there exists a tension between obedience and disobedience to their principle of survival and progress? More plainly still: though a capitalist economy and society can perish through disapproval of capitalism, can it survive without the presence of substantial disapproval? Would not a capitalist society which was 100 per cent approved by its members be bound to disappear?

The market mechanism is an instinctual one. Unlike the various alternatives proposed to it, it was not deliberately designed, still less created, though it can be more or less rejected, and though it can be analysed and studied, no government or ruler could, or would, impose it. The 'invisible hand' of Adam Smith's metaphor is – to pile another metaphor on top – the 'hand of Nature'. There is indeed a truth, if not in the sense intended, in the objurgation that the market is a 'jungle' and its rules the 'law of the jungle'; for the real jungle is a place not of disorder and confusion but of highly elaborate and intricate equilibria. It may be that the antipathy to this instinctual mechanism, which expresses itself in moral terms, is something fundamental to humanity, and perhaps not exclusively to humanity. It may even be that the antipathy is as indispensable as the instinctual mechanism itself. If so, no amount of the reasoned argument which the antipathy provokes will be sufficient to exorcise it.

Professor Acton's book is sub-titled 'An Ethical Exploration'. I have suggested that there is here a far vaster and more difficult region than we commonly imagine. Moral philosophy may have suggested the existence of this unknown region; but it is not to moral philosophy that the leadership of the exploration will fall.

New Statesman, 26 March 1971   *Claire Tomalin*

LIBERTY, EQUALITY, SORORITY

Kate Millett, like Germaine Greer, is good at stirring things up by overstating a case, and perhaps moderate feminists should give thanks for that, just as the suffragists had reason to be grateful to the suffragettes for focusing public attention, however much they might deplore rail-chaining, arson and suicide under a Derby Day horse. Mrs Pankhurst deserves her statue even if Mrs Fawcett's attitudes were more reasonable.

So there seems to be a case for extremism. But Mrs Pankhurst had an achievable end – the vote – whereas Kate Millett's long contribution to

current feminist thinking, *Sexual Politics*,* advocates changes that
mean women must stop *wanting* what in general they clearly do want at
the moment: family life. I wonder if the publicity the extremist wing of
feminism is courting and receiving at the moment does not risk
obscuring practical and possible issues under frivolous or lunatic
theories and demands. I hope not; it would be nice to see more pressures
for nursery schools and forget about 24-hours-a-day nurseries, which
are a bad idea.

Kate Millett's book arrives in England after she has already
conceded in America (*Time*, August 1970) that 'my book did overstate
the case, because nobody was listening. All I did was substantiate a
cliché which we all know – that it's a man's world.' In fact she does
much more than this; but the concession makes reasoned appraisal of
the book's attitudes and arguments rather tricky.

Miss Millett says she believes that the sexual relationship is a political
one, necessarily embodying a power struggle in which women are
always exploited even when they seem to be privileged. To demonstrate
this she chooses (somewhat arbitrarily) three main topics: Victorian
literature; what she calls the counter-revolution, involving the
imposition of Freud's ideas on female psychology by his followers and
popularisers; and a few selected 20th-century writers who concern
themselves with sex – D. H. Lawrence, Henry Miller, Mailer and Genet.

On the counter-revolution she is thorough and convincing, but has
little to add, except in the amassing of detail (and in factual chapters on
Nazi Germany and Soviet Russia), to what Eva Figes, Germaine Greer
and Betty Friedan have already said. I doubt if Englishwomen have
been affected by it to the same extent as American; working-class
women here are kept down by simple economic injustice, and educated
women rarely have the leisure for psychoanalysis or the inclination to
take seriously the women's magazines which give watered-down
Freudian messages about not competing. Still, it is probably
responsible for some entrenched male stupidity and some unnecessary
anxiety amongst women, and deserves all the knocking it gets. And for
sheer entertainment value, read Kate Millett's account of the American
social psychologist Orville G. Brim Jr's table of traits assignable to
male and female nursery school children: little boys are 'self-confident'
and 'competitive' whereas little girls are 'insistent on rights', 'jealous',
'exhibitionistic' and apparently without curiosity, ambition or tenacity.

If she had stuck to her discussion of these topics, she would have
produced a small, sharp additional weapon for the feminist armoury.
Unfortunately she feels impelled to pad out her book with huge sections

* *Sexual Politics* by Kate Millett. Hart-Davis (£2.50).

devoted to literary criticism. Much of it is good knockabout stuff – exit, bruised and limping, D. H. Lawrence, Henry Miller and Norman Mailer, nursing assorted reprehensible sexual fantasies – but not central to her argument. You may or may not feel these writers' attitudes are insulting to women; they are certainly not damaging in any fundamental sense. In fact, though it may not have been their intention, these three have probably contributed to the sexual emancipation of women.

Her discussion of Genet becomes distinctly disturbing, for the following reason: she offers us his account of homosexual relations (brutal and unloving ones at that) as though it could be equated with heterosexual love. But it can't be; the overwhelming majority of women in our society experience heterosexual love as a progression from exclusive preoccupation with a lover to a desire to bear children by him and rear them with him. And however unhappy family life may turn out to be, it is stretching analogy too far to see it in terms of the slavish submission of the young prison boy to the criminal who rapes and degrades him.

The analogy does work better when applied to Victorian England, when women were deliberately kept in sexual ignorance and financial dependence, and Miss Millett, expert on the period, often seems to be grounding her indignation on conditions and attitudes existing then. With relentless earnestness she takes us through *The Princess*, and excoriates Ruskin at great length for his essay 'Of Queen's Gardens', which idealised the housekeeping and charitable role thought proper for middle-class women by most people then. Ruskin had not the vision of Mill or Morris, but to do him justice he was very keen that girls should be educated, and spoke up for better treatment of governesses in order to improve standards. Curiously, Miss Millett does not mention Florence Nightingale's *Cassandra* essay in which she depicts the appalling agonies of frustration endured by a 'Daughter at Home' who wished to be working. But Miss Nightingale is an awkward figure for feminists; she refused to help John Stuart Mill in his campaign for suffrage, or to endorse the idea of women becoming doctors rather than nurses. She thought the general misery of the poor and the married women's property act mattered more than the vote, and though she changed her mind somewhat as she grew older, she was always unkind about 'the enormous Jaw about Women's Work'. Probably her own ultimate success in freeing herself from traditional feminine bondage made her impatient of the complaints and endeavours of those who found it more difficult; this type of arrogance is unattractive, but on the other hand it is still possible today to feel that many women bind themselves in chains voluntarily and then start complaining. It is not the wickedness of power-hungry men that makes women want to bear children.

Children are the crux of the problem for Kate Millett; she shares a hatred of the family with Florence Nightingale, who told Mrs Gaskell that:

if she had influence enough not a mother should bring up a child herself; there should be creches for the rich as well as the poor. If she had 20 children she would send them all to a creche, seeing, of course, that it was a well managed creche.

Thirty years after Miss Nightingale, and for somewhat different reasons, Engels made a similar pronouncement which provides Kate Millett with her inspiration:

With the transformation of the means of production into collective property, the monogamous family will cease to be the economic unit of society. The care and education of children becomes a public matter.

To which Miss Millett adds:

... for so long as every female, simply by virtue of her anatomy, is obliged, even forced, to be the sole or primary caretaker of childhood, she is prevented from being a free human being. The care of children, even from the period when the cognitive powers first emerge, is infinitely better left to the best trained practitioners of both sexes who have chosen it as a vocation.

In her world, who would choose such a vocation? Her blueprint for sexual revolution is founded on the idea that there is something inherently degrading in the maternal role, that child care is scarcely a human activity:

The modern nuclear family ... necessitates male supremacy by preserving specifically human endeavour for the male alone, while confining the female to menial labour and compulsory child care...

But unless she really believes that children can be brought up without individual care, the numbers of the population who will have to become 'trained practitioners' will need to equal the present number of subhumanly employed mothers.

For obvious reasons, this revolution is unlikely to take place; the ideas behind it are silly, not dangerous, because men and women are so disinclined to abandon the hopes they place in the family structure and attempt to rear children like battery chickens. Women are already partially protected from oppression by birth control, divorce, family allowances; equal pay and day nursery schools must be fought for; but what legislation can abolish the fact that those who wish to bear children do so at the cost of advancement in their other activities?

We waste talent and we educate insufficiently still; this applies to both sexes, more to women. But to say that males arrogate to themselves all human achievement, as Kate Millett does (in a paragraph that opens with a quotation from Hannah Arendt, scarcely a prime example of crushed femininity), is not true. To assert that the brutal sexual mores of the working class have now been taken up by the middle class, as she also claims, is untrue too, outside the theatre and fiction. It is far nearer the truth to say that, although irrational attitudes, economic oppression and poor education still make life difficult for women in English and American society, their lot is better than it has ever been and shows signs of improving steadily.

Even if one disagrees with many aspects of Kate Millett's thinking, it is possible to respect her desire that everyone should be free to express themselves as fully as possible, not crammed into a stereotype. Poor Valerie Solanas's SCUM manifesto, cheerily offered by Girodias as 'the Charter of all female revolutionaries', is a pathetic example of a distracted mind.* It will give comfort to those who believe that feminism is a pathological condition, product of hysteria, sexual bitterness or perversion. SCUM (in case you didn't know) is the Society for Cutting Up Men; Miss Solanas is famous for shooting Andy Warhol; her programme includes the total annihilation of the human race after the male sex has been properly humiliated. 'My contribution to the study of violence,' chirps the publisher; one didn't think somehow he was motivated by a pure love of feminine freedom in making this available to us.

Spectator, 17 July 1971   *Harold Wilson*

RAB

During the Spanish Civil War, the *News Chronicle* of December 8, 1938, Rab Butler tells us in his memoirs†

... was good enough to say I had excelled myself during the previous afternoon in the capacity of Stonewaller, 'while the Prime Minister sat silent'. I am portrayed as having gone through the long hour of questions, through three phases: first, determination combined with an air of injured innocence; second,

* *SCUM Manifesto* by Valerie Solanas. Olympia (25p).
† *The Art of the Possible* by R. A. Butler. Hamish Hamilton (£3.75).

friendliness with an implied appeal for mercy by the bowlers: third, righteous indignation. My most telling remark was thought to be, 'A certain incident has taken place and a certain answer was returned.' All this sounds more light-hearted in retrospect than it felt amid the passions of the time.

Throughout his book Rab shows that he still enjoys a joke against himself as much as he did in the House of Commons – we all remember the uninhibited, unsimulated chuckles of laughter when any of his opponents made an effective crack about him or his colleagues. But this quotation from page 74 of *The Art of the Possible* is just a little too characteristic of the book as a whole: he has a tendency to under-write the great occasions. Worse, Rab repeatedly fails to answer the bigger questions in the reader's mind: why was he so often in the position – as in the instance he quotes from the Spanish Civil War – of defending policies which were so basically indefensible; did he question them even in his own mind; did he ever seek to change them?

This is a disappointing book for one main reason. Though it is entertainingly written, with all the deft touches his contemporaries so enjoyed in Parliament, it fails to measure up to its subject – one of the outstanding public men and Parliamentary characters of our age. In giving the impression that things just happened to him, he is far too prone to understate how much events – and still more what his more flamboyant leader Harold Macmillan would refer to as 'tides of history' – owe to his contribution, to his persuasion and to his hard work. His personality and his achievements will inevitably go inadequately recorded if this book is the last word on Rab.

There is perhaps one exception to this. In one of the later chapters, he warms to the task of describing the reforms for which he was responsible in the working and policies of his party after 1945, a contribution as historically significant as Peel's revolution in the Tamworth Manifesto, if, sadly for the country – and his party – it has not survived for so long.

This book is disappointing, too, in failing to deal adequately and frankly with the two great turning-points of his political life – Suez and the selection of a successor to Anthony Eden, and the leadership crisis of October 1963.

There are hints of a partial dissociation in his mind from the lunacy of Suez, but no explanation why, feeling as he undoubtedly did, he did not press the issue to the limit. True, one could hardly have seen Rab banging the table, but he would have had powerful support. It was Kingsley Martin who explained the choice of Harold Macmillan as Prime Minister in terms of a reaction from a painful and sour hangover. After the inexplicable orgy of Suez, the Conservative party turned to a boon companion who bore more responsibility than any other for both the binge and the hangover, and rejected the man who had gone along with the company and tasted nothing stronger than tomato juice.

There were many, particularly among the younger members, among the forward-looking generation – of whom a great number owed their election and their personal adoption of the Conservative philosophy to Rab – who were looking to him for a lead he did not give. Perhaps he foresaw that the crisis would have effects going far beyond the immediate invasion and would ultimately engulf the leadership, for which he was one of the only two possible contenders – there was no credible third man. Did he fear it would count against him? Did he feel that the party should be given its head, or fear that the old taunt of Municheer would be hurled against him? If so, he gained little from it; on his own analysis he must have realised that the men of Suez, those who drew a totally false analogy between Nasser and Hitler, the time-servers, and the Whips, were those who stood to gain – and their guilt was total.

It is extraordinary, recalling how the House was misled, and even deceived, about the true facts – and conscious, as Rab must be, how much damaging evidence has been published since – that he is as silent on these questions as Harold Macmillan himself in his latest volume. Inconceivable as it is that Rab was in the inner circle who knew of all the manoeuvres and collusion, it is surprising that the word 'Villacoublay'* is absent from his index, as indeed, it was from that of Harold Macmillan's account. Rab would have done better – fifteen years after, and halfway to the operation of the thirty-year rule – to have made clear where he stood, and to have given his reaction to the disclosures which have become part of the literature of Suez.

Equally disappointing is his account of the second major crisis in his public career, the 1963 leadership struggle. It is certainly readable, and his account of what went on in those smoke-filled Blackpool rooms, and above all in those last hours when the decision was slipping away from him, adds a little to our knowledge of those great events. But only a little. Where Randolph Churchill in a few weeks recorded so much – almost all of it unchallenged – Rab in as many years has added so little. Except for one thing: the strange light he sheds on the mercurial Quintin Hogg. Not only the strange circumstances of the renunciation of his peerage, against Rab's advice, but his outburst over the telephone on the Thursday, October 17 – 'This simply won't do' – his 'characteristic

* The air-base outside Paris where French and British leaders prepared the Suez operation—K.A.

fury' the following, crucial morning, only to be followed by his acquiescence in Sir Alec's appointment later in the day.

This was undoubtedly the most traumatic period in Rab's public life.

It was unfortunate for him that Harold Macmillan, while too ill to continue in Downing Street, yet felt well enough to play a decisive role in the choice of his successor, having already told the sixty-one-year-old Rab, then two years younger than Macmillan had been on succeeding to the Premiership, that on age grounds he was better fitted to be kingmaker than king. It is difficult to escape the conclusion that Harold Macmillan's views on Rab's succession were not dissimilar from those of Clem Attlee on Herbert Morrison. But Clem was not, in the habit of leaving his fingerprints around.

Despite this, Rab fails in his book to provide any of the answers to the questions everyone was asking. Even more disappointing, he does not even mention the questions.

Could Rab, by refusing to serve under Sir Alec Douglas-Home, have prevented Harold Macmillan's nominee from taking over? For in these days it is a rare event if, when the monarch sends for a potential Prime Minister, the response is not a kissing of hands but an undertaking to inquire whether a Government could be formed: the question remained open. Rab's account gives the impression of a limited but dutiable* resentment. He clearly shared the doubts which so many of his senior colleagues felt. Even more he resented the manner in which the choice had been made. He was unsure about the number of backbenchers who would not bear him. Clearly there was a number who had it in for him, yet he could not know how many – it would be interesting to know their quantity and reasons – and he seemed too ready to regard them as adequate in numbers to block his appointment. But he lifts the veil sufficiently to indicate that he had reason to feel that the soundings taken had been prejudiced by the manner in which at least some of the Whips had put the question. Under direction? And, if so, whose? He gives no answer, while suggesting that the attitude of the Whips' Office was decisive.

The best comment on the whole operation, which Rab perhaps would, with greater frankness, endorse, was that expressed at the time by the then Conservative commentator, William Rees-Mogg, in the *Sunday Times*: that the Conservatives had ceased to be gentlemen while not yet becoming democrats.

This raises another question which must be asked. Had Humphry Berkeley succeeded not in 1965 but in 1963 in persuading the Conservative parliamentary party to accept an elective system on a

* 'Liable to [excise] duty' (OED)—K.A.

change in the leadership, what would the results have been? Since we do not know the real strength of those who would not have Rab at any price, it is impossible to estimate what the outcome would have been. At least it is arguable that an indecisive result on the first ballot would have put Rab in a position to exercise a decisive influence on the choice of any alternative. Nor is it possible to estimate, if Rab had been elected, how the knife-edge election of 1964 would have gone. It might have been a Conservative majority which was called upon to face the implication of an £800 million payments deficit with a majority of less than half a dozen.

Another unanswered question, and Rab was undoubtedly right not to raise this, was what might have happened had Labour won by a larger majority so that the 1964 Parliament would have begun with every prospect of a full term. At least one detached observer, who by definition could not be described as a Senior or any other rank of Conservative, felt at the time that the Conservatives would have been wise to choose Rab as an interim leader, to guide his party in a 1945-type reappraisal after thirteen years of office, and to retain his post long enough for the young lions to fight it out among themselves and enable the clear successor to emerge. But Rab's name had been blackened by the unscrupulous exploitation by the Tories of some unguarded comments to a *Daily Express* journalist – now gone to higher things – on a train. In the event, Rab's acceptance of Downing Street's offer of the nomination to Trinity closed this option for the Conservatives.

1956 and 1963, then, are disappointing chapters in this book. But though the work as a whole fails to live up to the stature and mystery that was Rab, it is still an entrancing account of a long period of history. Telling us so little of the Rab of the crises, it tells us a great deal of the essential Rab of the first twenty-five years of his Parliamentary life. We learn more than we could ever have known of the influence on him of his early years in India, and of his intellectual inheritance. We knew – but are now able to confirm from his own words – what his domestic life gave to him. We learn what Saffron Walden and the wider Essex community meant to him – as much, even, as Stockton meant to Harold Macmillan.

The present political generation, and the historian, learn more than most of us realise about all that went into the fights over the Government of India Bill, and, surprising from the point of view of later comment, about the Olympian stature his colleagues accorded to Stanley Baldwin, and the evidence of the sureness of his touch – the victory of his Fabian strategy, until the challenge of the dictators and Baldwin's inadequate response, produced a new assessment.

The other fascinating part of this book is Rab's very personal account of his educational reforms, though even here his meiotic form of expression underrates the extent of his achievement, particularly in the negotiations on denominational schools – even more when one reads how the 1944 Act was pushed through in the face of a clear and explicit veto from Winston Churchill at the height of his wartime power.

His response to this veto was the one clear evidence in his public life that he had the steel to decide that an issue on which he was utterly determined was not to be limited by conventional notions of the 'art of the possible'.

For those are the words he has chosen to cover the whole of his massive contribution to his country's history. That they represent his definition of politics is proved again and again in these pages. It may be that this was because his early ministerial life was at a junior level in an age when compromise on big issues of principle, and international principle at that, dominated the stage. He might have been more fortunate if his first ministerial appointment, like that of Harold Macmillan, had been in May 1940, and not in 1932, or if his role at the time of Munich had been only that of an umbrella-carrying PPS not a Minister of the Crown.

When the great divide came in 1956, and again in 1963, he appeared committed by over-long experience, and perhaps by a sense of party loyalty which proved singularly ill-rewarded, to interpreting the art of the possible in excessively limited terms. Too often he set his sights too low. Too frequently he failed to ask what the possible might be, given determination to enlarge its horizons and to inspire others, as he was capable of doing, with what those horizons might mean.

Public life in Rab's generation has shown, as in all other ages, that while political parameters can never extend beyond what is possible, the greatest achievements have been recorded in the days when there were those who decided that sometimes it is necessary to set one's sights on the impossible. It may not always be achieved, certainly most times it will fail of achievement, but most of our history has been made by those who tried.

New Statesman, 30 July 1971   *Alan Brien*

TEN RULES FOR ENJOYING HOLIDAYS

Well, the title is probably wrong to begin with. There are not 10 rules for enjoying holidays. There is not one rule. A holiday is something no reasonable person expects to enjoy, except in retrospect. Like having your appendix out, or going on a health food diet, or being sent away to school, or serving in the armed forces, or swimming in cold water, or reading articles on the Common Market, or having your teeth scaled, it often makes a good story afterwards. Or at least, you *think* it makes a good story afterwards. Your listeners are just waiting until you finish to feed in their good story in revenge. But, at the time, the best you can hope for is to survive, and endure, with a brave face. (Your brave face is that one, radiant with sunburn, ascetic with sleeplessness, ennobled by poverty, which appears in the top right-hand corner of other people's snapshots.)

A holiday means being condemned to do all the things you most hate doing the rest of the year – asking the way of strangers, studying time-tables, over-tipping or under-tipping, travelling in crowds, making small-talk about what you do for a living, wondering where the children have got to, above all, taking endless decisions. You become a one-man bureaucracy, always balancing the budget, signing forms, producing documents, battling with the balance of payments problem, reading the small print, holding conferences, laying down rules. It is almost like being Harold Wilson for a month. But who will buy your memoirs?

The first rule then must be – *Don't Think It's Going To Be Fun.* A holiday is just a continuation of business by other means. You're still in the rat-race at 90 degrees in the shade, manufacturing anecdotes for home consumption, exporting lies on the backs of postcards, siting the camera so that it just misses registering the cooling tower, the electric power lines, the police barracks and the enamelled tin hoardings. You've got your status to consider. Don't let up – there are 11 months left in which to recover. Expect the worse, and you may have got one forecast right.

Rule two – *Always Take the First Alternative.* The sixth restaurant won't be any better. The tenth will be ruinously expensive. And the eleventh will be closed for its annual holidays. Anyway, your sandals are killing you. The next train doesn't exist. The nearest beach has many advantages – for one thing, it's nearer. The further you go, the more you have to cart with you, and the heavier it will grow on the way back. So perhaps you can find a place without another living soul in sight and you know what? You've forgotten to bring any matches. Commercialisation is something you want to get away from until you realise you are now the only possible source of salt, butter, wine, cigarettes, water, newspaper, books, suntan lotion, Kleenex, sticking plaster, sanitary towels and petrol. You are in a monopoly position. You've cornered the market. And you can't even make a profit.

Rule three – *Stay In One Spot*. It is better to cavil than arrive. Getting there is half the agony. You don't want to be the tenderfoot, the tyro, and the dude everywhere. At least here, you'll be the oldest foreign resident within 10 days. The more places you visit, the more unforgettable experiences you will have missed. 'You mean you didn't see the snake-charmers in the courtyard of the Sultan's Palace? The dawn from the peak of I Promessi Sposi? The baroque altarpiece by the Master of *Gesundheitspflege*?'

Rule four – *Be Yourself*. One sign of the unnatural pressures exerted upon otherwise balanced people by going on holiday is the sort of friends you make while away from it all. What with the sirocco, the mistral and the monsoon, Ramadan and the period of mourning for the dead dictator, the state of emergency and the cholera scare, communal riots and police round-ups, you will chum up with anybody who isn't in uniform and expecting a small commission payable in advance. Avoid making conversation about powered lawnmowers, *au pair* girls, unit trusts, London bus routes, souvenir shops, and comical mistranslations in guidebooks, unless these are topics upon which you already pride yourself. When exchanging addresses and telephone numbers, make some small, but vital, error of detail which will discourage your desperate relationship being later re-activated. If you are one of the pale people, do not hope to be fried brown, like a chip, on the beach. Women seem to have a natural aptitude for accommodating to the horizontal. No normal man can lie on his front without finding sand seeping inside his trunks and tunnelling up his nose, or on his back without his hands draining of blood and his head becoming numb. Visit the Uffizi as often as you do the National Gallery, the cathedral as frequently as you do Westminster Abbey. Remember that however much the banknotes look like cocoa labels, they are not fairy money.

Rule five – *Beware of Appearing Too Expert*. It is all right boasting in your local about your longing for baby octopus boiled in its mother's ink, sheep's eyes basted with fresh camel's blood, mice baked *en croute*, or locusts preserved in honey. Here, your bluff may be called when it turns up as the dish of the day. Then they may not remember you in that Andalusian village where you were so much part of the native scene two years ago that they begged you to stand for *Alcalde*.* Every tourist has fond memories of his favourite waiter, but there have been a thousand bottoms in that cafe seat since last you were there. Don't translate too literally – it is a reliable maxim that the English word which most resembles the foreign word is never the right one. Don't take short cuts, especially in the *casbah*. Be prepared for negative feedback if you must

* Means 'mayor' actually – K.A.

make jokes about the Mafia, the evil eye, the Nazis, the Pope, the water supply, the Colonels, the local football team. Drink anything alcoholic, but don't open your mouth in the Mediterranean. Keep reminding yourself it is not a crime to be recognised as an Englishman abroad.

Rule six. Well, I can't think of anymore actually. But who wants an article entitled Five Rules for Enjoying Holidays? A final thought – it is your holiday, not the neighbours', or the travel writers', or Kodak developing labs'. You don't have to pass an examination on it, or leave a permanent record for posterity, when you get back. The fewer photographs you take, the more you see. Eventually the most important rule for enjoying a holiday may be not to feel you have to prove you did so.

Spectator, 31 July 1971   *Paul Foot*
HAROLD'S PARTY

Mr Harold Wilson dedicates this book* 'To the hundreds of thousands of members of the Labour party whose efforts and idealism created the Government of 1964–70 and who, in dark days and brighter ones, sustained it with their unwavering loyalty.'

Hundreds of thousands of Labour party members there may be, but there are at least two hundred thousand less than when Mr Wilson's government first took office in 1964. At the Blackpool Labour Party Conference in September 1965 – the first full conference of the Labour government – 531 constituency Labour parties were represented, with an affiliated voting strength of 871,000. Five years later, at Blackpool once more, with their Government in Opposition, 492 constituencies were represented, with 625,000 votes.

The real picture is probably even worse. Local Labour parties must affiliate to a minimum of 1,000 members if they want to be represented at conference. This minimum affiliation, which in most cases greatly exaggerates the paying (let alone active) party membership, accounts for the bulk of the 1970 representation from constituencies. The truth is that during the period of the first majority Labour government to hold office with an impregnable Parliamentary majority in peacetime conditions, the 'efforts and idealism' of the Labour rank and file went into an unprecedented and apparently irreversible decline.

There is no evidence that Harold Wilson and his Ministers, when in

* *The Labour Government 1964–70: a personal record* by Harold Wilson. Weidenfeld and Michael Joseph (£4.80).

office, concerned themselves very much with this situation. In Opposition, however, the Labour leaders must turn once more to their supporters in an attempt to galvanise 'efforts and idealism' into a 'crusade' which will once again return Labour to office. Those small parts of Mr Wilson's gargantuan memoir which are devoted to political analysis are tilted sharply to the Left. In recounting his reactions to crises in currency valuation, Vietnam, Rhodesia, immigration and so on, Mr Wilson is at pains to assure his readers that the man who spent six years in Downing Street imitating Stanley Baldwin was the same Yorkshire socialist who resigned with Nye Bevan in 1951.

Mr Wilson tells us that, when, at the outset of his Government, he was pressed by Lord Cromer and the City of London to cut back public expenditure to save the pound, he threatened a general election unless Cromer persuaded the central bankers to bail Britain out. He tells us too that the Labour government's support for the American government's policies in Vietnam was prompted solely by the desire to 'get the parties to the conference table'. On Rhodesia, or on immigration, Mr Wilson does not spare the reader the most unctuous expressions of his belief in multi-racialism.

The effect of all this new-found radicalism can be judged, at least to some extent, from Mr Wilson's record itself. We learn that Lord Cromer got £3,000 million from the central bankers after Mr Wilson's election threat. Before long, however, Mr Wilson discovered the accuracy of his own forecast during the 1964 campaign:

You cannot go cap in hand to the central bankers and maintain your freedom of action. . . . The central bankers will before long be demanding that Britain puts her house in order, and their idea of an orderly house usually comes to mean vicious inroads into the Welfare State and a one-sided pay pause.

The cuts and deflations of 1965, 1966, 1967 and 1968 are blamed, correctly enough, on speculators but nowhere does Mr Wilson explain why he did not, or could not, take the speculators on.

Likewise, the long months of support for the American government in Vietnam reached their climax in February 1967 when, after hours of delicate negotiation with Mr Kosygin, Mr Wilson was on the verge of a diplomatic coup. But all hopes of a 'conference table' settlement were shattered – not by the Russians, but by the American government.

The book's long passages on Rhodesia are dogged by similar contradiction. After UDI, Mr Wilson (in a passage for some reason unquoted in his memoir) made it plain that he regarded the very suggestion of negotiation with Mr Smith as 'the product of the most woolly-minded thinking I have yet come across.' It was, he said, like dealing 'with a burglar.'

Contempt for Smith and his illegal regime pervades all Mr Wilson's Rhodesian passages. Why, therefore, from early in 1966 to the autumn of 1968 did he keep a negotiating line open to Smith, and twice meet the 'burglar' on British ships of war? There is an attempt at an answer:

I told him [Premier Obote of Uganda] that public opinion in Britain would expect us to make, at any rate, one final effort to reach an accommodation with Smith, provided that it embodied in full the guarantees called for in the six principles. That attempt must be made....

How did Mr Wilson thus gauge public opinion? And how does he justify his attempts to 'accommodate' the racialist regime not on one occasion, but on two? How does he explain the fact that the terms offered to Smith on 'Tiger' (and even more so on 'Fearless') made nonsense of all six principles except the last which was included (by Wilson himself) solely to comfort the white minority? The 'Tiger' terms made majority rule more difficult even than the 1961 Whitehead Constitution; it gave no 'guarantee' (beyond mere words) for the 'entrenched clauses'; it left the job of assessing the 'acceptability' of the proposals to a Royal Commission chaired by the Rhodesian Chief Justice, Sir Hugh Beadle, whose duplicity shocked even Mr Wilson.

The answer is that Wilson explains and justifies none of these things. He was, he tells us at length, very angry indeed when African leaders were not properly fed on the one day he met them, but he has nothing at all to say about his willingness to sell the future of at least a generation of Rhodesian Africans in the vain hope of a diplomatic 'triumph'.

The account of the Labour government's approach to racial matters nearer home follows the same pattern. There is a long quotation from a Wilson speech which was made in the spring of 1968 in indignant response to Mr Enoch Powell's lugubrious fantasies about immigration. Less space is devoted to the Labour government's handling of the Kenyan Asians question only two months before Mr Powell's 'rivers of blood' speech. Not even an attempt is made at justification for the (Kenyan Asian) Immigration Act, 1968. Wilson writes that, in the House of Commons, 'The Opposition ... cravenly decided to abstain.'

This is nonsense. The Conservatives supported the Government throughout on the Immigration Bill. In the debate on the second reading, on February 27, 1968, Mr Maudling from the Opposition front bench announced his party's support for the Bill, and he, Mr Heath and Mr Hogg (then the party spokesman on Home Affairs) joined Mr Wilson and his colleagues in the lobby. In an attempt to deflect attention from his Government's racist legislation, Mr Wilson blithely distorts the record.

This lack of politics, this refusal to outline any overall political strategy, extends throughout the volume. To expect more was, perhaps, a trifle ambitious. But at least the reader of such a long and richly-rewarded account could expect some *information*. At least the self-congratulation and lists of legislation could be illuminated with gobbets of gossip.

Unhappily, not so. It is not until page 473 that Mr Wilson tells us: 'I have not felt it appropriate in general to draw back the veil which rightly covers the detailed transactions of a Cabinet.' So we do not know who opposed the European application, who supported arms sales to South Africa (apart from George Brown), who supported devaluation in July 1966 (apart from George Brown), who opposed the 'Tiger' settlement in Rhodesia, who opposed 'In Place of Strife'. We cannot even know why Richard Marsh was sacked in the reshuffle of 1969.

I have discovered, for the record, three pieces of interesting information in 790 pages: They are: (1) that Sir Basil Smallpiece offered the Labour government half the equity in Cunard at a knock-down price (it was not accepted); (2) that Miss Margaret Herbison resigned from the Government in 1967 because a proposed increase in pensions was too low, and (3) that Arrow Enterprises, a fund-raising organisation, was due to receive 110 per cent of the proceeds of the fund-raising dinner to boost Common Market propaganda at Guildhall in July 1969. Mr Wilson and Mr Thorpe refused to attend until Arrow was offered instead a flat-rate fee (which is not disclosed).

Without politics, then, and without information, we are left with the picture of a devoted and tireless administrator darting around the country and the world in a constant, losing battle against the buffetings of speculators, employers, trade union 'activists', an unscrupulous and opportunist Opposition, a hostile press and television (Mr Wilson congratulates himself unstintingly on the worst of his many appalling public appointments – that of Lord Hill to the chairmanship of the BBC Board of Governors – but cannot resist persistent sniping at the BBC for not affording him adequate publicity).

This is not the picture painted by the Conservative press of an evil scheme, concerned solely with personal advantage. On the contrary, Mr Wilson's instincts are kindly, friendly, humanitarian and sentimental (readers interested in displays of sentimentality should refer to the Wilsons' visit to the Pope and, particularly, to Mr Wilson's acquisition of Manchester United buttons for General Gowon, Prime Minister of Nigeria). These instincts, however, are subordinated to the supreme quality of which Mr Wilson has boasted on more than one occasion: his pragmatism. This pragmatism stems from an obsession with office, rather than with power. There can be no doubt, for instance, that Mr Wilson would have preferred Hubert Humphrey to win the American Presidential election of 1968, but when Richard Nixon was elected, Mr Wilson greeted and treated him with unflagging obsequiousness.

One revealing passage concerns a Cabinet reshuffle in which Richard Marsh was asked to move from the Ministry of Power to Transport:

Barbara Castle had to have a keen successor and, in view of the public interest in everything to do with motoring and road safety, one with a good sense of public relations. I was surprised to see how sorry he (Marsh) was at being asked to move; most would have regarded it as promotion. When he asked about the constitutional position of a minister's being asked to change, I had to tell him . . . that if the captain asked a fielder to move from square leg to cover point, then that was exactly where he had to move.

The very idea that any of his team should be more interested in the job he was doing than in 'promotion' or 'public relations' was incomprehensible.

Try as he might to rekindle some sense of socialist purpose in the party which brought him to power in 1964, Mr Wilson cannot free himself from the bonds of his own pragmatism. Whatever his administrative and rhetorical skill, and whatever his ability to survive in high places (no one should be foolish enough to write him off for a long time yet) the plain fact is that for the 'hundreds and thousands' of members of the Labour party, and, more importantly, for the future of socialism, Mr Wilson's administration was an unmitigated disaster. His book tells his supporters nothing about how they are to avoid a repeat performance.

New Statesman, 26 May 1972   *Unsigned*

THE LOST LEADER

Mr Harold Wilson has now been Leader of the Labour party for approaching a decade. Few of his predecessors came to the job with greater promise; none was ever handed a richer opportunity. The qualities of resourcefulness and resilience he originally displayed as

Leader of the Opposition will always remain on the record. Certainly no start could have been more propitious.

Yet no one has any prescriptive right to remain Leader of the Labour party in perpetuity. Unfortunately it is one of Mr Wilson's least attractive characteristics that, whenever criticism is raised against him, he should instantly smell a 'plot' or claim to detect a 'conspiracy'. The truth of the present situation is quite the reverse. Far from being threatened by a 'plot' – or undermined by any 'conspiracy' – Mr Wilson's leadership is underpinned at the moment by a curious form of paralysis that seems to be affecting the entire Labour movement. Mr Wilson, it is said, fully intends to lead the Labour party into the next election and – like it or lump it – that is a fact of life which his followers must accept.

But why should they? It is not, after all, as if there is anything in the history of Mr Wilson's last premiership to give him any special charge on the party's conscience. There may be no purpose now in raking over all his errors and failures – though their variety is manifold and their number legion. What, however, cannot help but be disquieting is the apparent equanimity with which his leading parliamentary colleagues still seem to contemplate at least the theoretical possibility of his becoming Prime Minister once more. Unless they too have become victims of self-deception they must know in their hearts that as things were before, so they would be again.

It might, admittedly, be different if Mr Wilson had ever shown the slightest sign of contrition or hint of repentance for the trial by ordeal (right down to his passive acquiescence in Roy Jenkins's tragically anti-socialist 1970 budget) to which he subjected the entire Labour movement during the nearly six years that he held office. But what has he done? Consciously or not, he has persistently tried to force the whole party to join him in the prison camp of his own political record. Even in the Commons he has become increasingly incapable of making the simplest intervention without seeking to justify – however vainly – the memory of some past misdeed. And on occasion he has gone even further.

Over Vietnam, for example, as Prime Minister he did not so much subject the Labour party to an endurance test as compel it to go over an assault course. Year after year the Labour party conference would pass resolutions condemning US policy; and year after year Mr Wilson, with an effortless consciousness of his own superiority, would simply ignore them. Even today it is doubtful if he has begun to understand the enormity of the affront that he delivered to the British Left. Certainly only a political leader with either a casual indifference to, or a callous disregard for, the feelings of his followers could have done what Mr Wilson did last year. Or has everyone forgotten that a year ago this month he actually went on a special expedition to America in order to go and stay with ex-President Johnson – who suitably rewarded him by announcing in public that he was his 'old and dear friend'?

Whatever may be the case at its parliamentary summit, at its base in the constituencies the Labour party has always been an almost superhumanly patient and forbearing body. Unfortunately, its forbearance is not shared by the electorate at large – and especially by younger voters whose support Labour must have if it is ever to win power again. For them, and with some justice, Mr Wilson stands today as the principal apostle of cynicism, the unwitting evangelist of disillusion. There have been just too great a number of tawdry compromises, too regular a series of clumsy attempts at vindication, too relentless a succession of political *pas de deux* danced solo. We say it with reluctance but we believe it to be true. Mr Wilson has now sunk to a position where his very presence in Labour's leadership pollutes the atmosphere of politics.

New Statesman, 30 June 1972   *Ruth Hall*

UNNATURAL BREAK

A voice telephoned saying they would just *love* to make a film in our house. Naturally they would. In the new Hampstead Californian glass-and-aluminium lean-to tradition, it is a triumph of advanced architectural creativity. Even the roof leaks. Carpeted throughout in what the trade calls 'shag', split-levelled by lethal stairs and unprotected balconies and littered with harpsichords, it is cinematically suited to both blue Grüppensex thrillers and tender evocations of the love-life of J. S. Bach.

'How much?' I demanded dulcetly.

'Fifty a day, and breakages.'

'Hmm...'

'All right, seventy-five.'

'I'll think about it,' I said, untruthfully.

Troubles, Shakespeare said, come not as single spies but in battalions. This lot came as single spies first of all, working up to battalion level gradually through scouting parties and platoons. As I blearily opened the door at 8 a.m. on Shooting Day, a whole army of producers, directors and actors burst through the breach. Behind them stretched ranks of cameramen, lighting engineers and clapper loaders, their rear brought up by a supply-train of tea-urns and crates of sandwiches.

Obviously, it was either *Hamlet* or *War and Peace*. Not being proud, I offered to be an extra in the Battle of Borodino sequence. PA Penelope looked a bit guilty. 'Oh, I thought I told you,' she said. 'It's a television commercial for Spanish red wine. *Terribly* full-bodied. Mummy buys it. 68p a bottle.' Well at least it wasn't dog food. Within seconds, the whole place was crammed, a nightmare party consisting entirely of unknown and uninvited guests. Sofas were wheeled out into the fishpond to make way for cameras, the kitchen brimmed with technicians drinking tea out of paper cups, and Wardrobe was ironing furiously in the study. The telephone rang. 'Tell Jeremy,' a voice said, 'that it's 108 inches and not 114.'

I fled to the bathroom for sanctuary. It was full of a large actor, reading Virginia Woolf and having his hair cut. 'I adore *The Waves*, don't you?' he said cheerily. 'Must be my *mood* at the moment.' Even the musicians' gallery was not sacrosanct. Supine on the polystyrene-granule-filled sausage sofas with which we like to moderate a fine collection of early keyboard instruments, a producer gazed through droopy eyes at Natasha, Jane and Annette. They were being tarred and feathered by Make-Up. False eyelashes fell thick as leaves in Vallombrosa, a fine coating of Rachel No 2 settled over the fortepiano and, through gossamer chiffon, liberated breasts stuck out like chapel hat-pegs.

'Lovely tits, dear,' the producer said wearily, 'but you'll have to do something with your hair.' 'It's so *thick*,' Natasha wailed complacently.

Now, I yield to no one in my aspirations. Convinced that a Schopenhauer revival is just round the corner, I scatter carefully-thumbed copies of *The World as Will and Idea* all over the harpsichords. I was quite upset when Props contemptuously replaced them with *Modern Primitives*, Sir K. Clark and other glossies considered more suitable for aspirant Spanish wine-bibbers. Worse still, louvred drapes were brought in to cover up the brutalist glass walls, and a tinkling mobile, disastrously NW5 rather than NW3, blossomed over the dining-table.

Against this background of rejigged reality, a smart dinner party was to take place. The main protagonist is 'a saturnine, good-looking, slick fast talker, fast mover, obviously keen on the ladies.' A man of the world, he sniffs suspiciously at the wine proffered by his casually but elegantly dressed hosts, and tastes it. Yes! A glimmer of approval

gradually widens into downright ecstasy: 'Torero!' (let us call it).
Almost Sophoclean in its inevitability.

It is, however, no easy task selling cheap Spanish red wine to a nation
of beer-drinkers. Rupert, our main guest, was the first to go under.
Though ever so saturnine, and wearing a lovely brown velvet suit, his
grasp on reality was much too firm.

'Ugh.' He gagged resignedly at the 13th take. 'Cut. Look, darling,'
the director said, 'All I want is *a dawning smile of appreciation*. For
God's sake.'

The dénouement was particularly tense. Around a table groaning
under piles of delectable, fresh-sprayed vegetables and a crown roast of
lamb from Harrods (uncooked to give a better colour on your screens)
the six guests despondently munched cheese sandwiches.

'All right, start rabbiting, everyone!,' the director said. 'Right now,
it's all happiness, joy, merriment, OK? Action! Come on, *chat*, damn
you! Annette, lean back. Jane, talk to Donald. Donald, pull the cork
out. Rabbit, *rabbit*, everybody! Happiness and gaiety. *Drink*, for God's
sake. Natasha, lean forward, darling, let's see your lovely tits. Look, my
love it just doesn't *work* unless you look happy. Once more, please.'

Towards midnight, we got on to close-ups. I had long ago decided to
join them, there being too many to beat. One by one we crept upstairs to
deaden our tastebuds with legitimately-opened bottles of Torero. Well,
somebody has to drink it. Fancy, I said, weeks of preparation,
regiments of people, 15 hours' shooting and £18,000, repeat £18,000
for 30 seconds of cheap red plonk on the telly.

Spectator, 26 August 1972   *T. E. Utley*
THE GREAT ILLUSION

No prizes will be offered for a correct prediction of the outcome of Mr
Whitelaw's conference of the Northern Irish political parties at the end
of next month. It is predestined, one might almost say scheduled, to fail.
Its function is ritualistic. It is designed to meet the requirement that
every chance of reaching a negotiated settlement should manifestly be
seen to have been exhausted before, as is inevitable, a settlement is
imposed by Britain.

Of course, it meets this requirement only in the barest and most
formal way. It is nothing short of fantastic to suppose that a conference
of politicians elected in Ulster four years ago is likely to represent
current Ulster opinion. Many of these politicians, the whole of the

SDLP and Alliance contingents for example, have changed their political labels since they were elected. In the last four years, Ulster has been engaged not only in a bloody civil war but in a passionate debate about the foundations of politics. New parties and new movements have emerged and there have been tentative flirtations between historic enemies. Anyone who really wanted to know what Ulster thought today would wait upon elections.

Mr Whitelaw's solution, however, already exists. It consists of a number of unchallenged assumptions on which the whole of British policy towards Ulster has for some time rested. The first and most elementary of these (it represents nothing more than a solemn resolution to abstain from doing what it is physically impossible to do) is that the Protestant population of the north cannot be simply handed over to the Republic. This cuts out Irish unity within any calculable period. The second is that the solution must contain no ingredient directly offensive to any of the sacred cows of non-violent Irish republicanism. This means in practice that the settlement must be patently if not professedly temporary, that is must leave the door open to peaceful unification and that it must not, in the first instance at least, return the control of internal security to any assembly dominated by the elected majority.

The one common element in the political programmes of all interested Irish parties (Unionists, Catholic opposition and Mr Lynch) is the existence of some sort of regional assembly. Out, therefore, must also go the logical, Powellite alternative to Irish unity – total integration in the United Kingdom. How many formal gestures of negotiation Mr Whitelaw may feel it necessary to make before his masterly compromise is announced cannot be foreseen; but the terms of the compromise are already plain. There will be no return to the imperial pomposities of Stormont; no more virtual county councillors strutting about calling themselves Right Honourables; but there will be a regional assembly comparable in some ways with the Greater London Council and charged with substantial duties in such matters as health, housing and education which, with their charming naïvety about all things Irish, British politicians regard as pleasantly uncontroversial.

Some sort of intellectual backing for this compromise is supplied by a study just published under the title *The Ulster Debate* by the Institute for the Study of Conflict*. It is a helpful little book which, without saying anything decisive, gives a courteous acknowledgement to every opinion, wise or foolish, which has been thrown up about Ulster in the last four years. Its only excursion into the realms of sheer political

* *The Ulster Debate*. Bodley Head (95p).

lunacy is given unfortunate prominence in an appendix contributed by Sir Frederick Catherwood who, as a former Director-General of the NEDC, speaks with authority on the pathology of moribund institutions. His quaint little idea is to provide that the new regional parliament shall not be able to enact any laws at all without the approval of a two-thirds majority. To do him credit he does envisage the possibility that under such a system the republican opposition would block virtually all legislation. If that were to happen, he would allow an appeal to Westminster. By this means, Direct Rule would undoubtedly be preserved, though in a form rather more productive of administrative anarchy, hostility in Ulster and exasperation at Westminster than the present version has been.

Oddly enough, this strange proposal (from which the group's rapporteur, Mr Moss, politely disassociates himself) appears as the climax to a book which shows real if intermittent understanding of a few crucial facts about Ulster. The first of these is that the civil war is not simply going to end but is going to remain at the very least latent and more probably sporadic for a very long time, a time which it would be more prudent to measure in decades than in years. Just as the progress towards reconciliation and smooth government will fluctuate with the successes and failures of terrorism, so the prospect of containing and subduing terrorism will depend largely on the strength and efficiency of political institutions. What a country in a state of perennial civil strife needs is not the bland assurance that all possibilities are open, that no doors are shut, that discussion is forever open-ended; what it needs is the certainty of political limits which will be enforced against all comers.

Britain neither wants to provide this framework of security for Ulster indefinitely nor is capable of doing so — two facts again which Mr Moss fully understands. It is unthinkable, for instance, that Northern Ireland could be effectively governed for the next half-century without at least the access to emergency powers, such as the power to create special courts and to intern, which the Republic has always found it necessary to keep on its statute book.

The inescapable Hobbesian inference is that the majority in Northern Ireland must be permitted and equipped to supply its own internal security. Many fear its own obvious capacity to do so; none can rationally doubt it. The premise of British policy must therefore be the need to restore something stronger not weaker than Stormont, something less vulnerable to the weakness, ineptitude, ignorance, mental confusion and political dishonesty of the modern Conservative party at Westminster as well as to the hypocrisy of the Labour party and the corrupt bargains with Irish rebels on which that party's electoral strength largely depends.

It might indeed be thought profitable for Britain to grant dominion status plus a handsome subsidy to Ulster and wash her hands of the whole tiresome business. The objection to this course of action is nonetheless valid for being purely moral. We have an obligation to the Catholic minority of Ulster from which neither the violence of a substantial part of that minority nor the propensity of almost all of it to lie about the oppressions to which in the past it has been subjected can absolve us. That obligation can only be discharged by entrenching all such minority rights as are compatible with stable government (including of course the franchise) in statutes at Westminster.

This indeed would not be adequate if anything like the past hegemony of the Unionist Party in Ulster were to be restored; but that is already irretrievably shattered. The introduction of proportional representation at elections, the birth of new parties, the internal divisions of the Unionists, all make its re-establishment impossible.

Of course, to this kind of realistic solution there is one overwhelming political obstacle. Would it not amount to reviving something very like the old Stormont? Would it not mean taking sides? Would it not mean positively refusing to add more to the concessions already extorted by violence and civil disobedience? Would it not look something like a return to Metternich and the principle of legitimacy?

For the past 150 years, radicals have successfully sold to the English conservative mind the axiom that no revolution must ever be allowed wholly or even substantially to fail, that victory is only rendered morally tolerable when it is followed by the surrender of the victor. The application of that principle in Ireland today can produce only anarchy and tyranny, but after all it is also being applied in Britain on a smaller scale and with what in the end are likely to be similar consequences. One day we shall deserve and get our Whitelaw.

Spectator, 30 September 1972   *Sandy Gall*
CONGO AND UGANDA

When they ran us up that hill and the big black soldier with a heavy automatic (a bit like the old Bren) kept jabbing me in the back with it, I thought: 'Here we go again.' It also crossed my mind that the only reason they were making us run was to find a pretext for the phrase favoured by so many executioners: 'Shot while trying to escape.' So I kept running as slowly as possible and my tormentor kept thumping me in the back with the muzzle of his weapon. But as I ran, trying to keep control of myself, trying to interpret his instructions, which were shouted in Swahili, trying to run fast enough not to get jabbed, and at the same time slow enough not to get shot, I realised with a dreadful hollow feeling in the stomach that I had been through all this once before, 12 years ago, and that I had no desire to repeat the performance.

The disadvantage in having had an almost parallel experience in the Congo (with, as it happens, George Gale, before he rose to editorial eminence, and a former BBC friend, Dickie Williams) was that I knew in advance how unpleasant the whole thing was likely to be. On the other hand this meant the terrors were more or less predictable for me, whereas for my young companion, Nick Moore of Reuters, the whole thing was an uncharted sea of despair. In the Congo we were arrested because we pitched up in the middle of a battle between Central Government forces from Leopoldville, as it was then, and the secessionists in the Kasai. We did a risky thing, and given the current atmosphere of hysteria about Belgian 'spies' it was not altogether surprising that we should be under suspicion. We were taken to an Army camp and held prisoner in a small room which soon became full of mostly drunken soldiers, who helped themselves to our watches, wallets etc. Our socks and shoes were removed – a trick that was to be repeated in Uganda. It seems that without his socks and shoes a white man will not be able to run very far. But looking back on that Congo experience which could easily have led to physical assault and finally a pull of the trigger, it strikes me now that the violence there was haphazard; whereas in Uganda today it is much more disciplined and therefore more dangerous. The Congo army was a murderous rabble; the Uganda army, thanks to British training, is a murderous machine, a Black Mafia with clearly defined chains of command, aided and supported by plain clothes *Tontons Macoute* one of whom carried out my arrest.

If one takes the long view it is clear that Uganda is going through the same convulsive anti-colonialist *crise* that the Congo suffered in 1960–64. Then it was Belgians who were the target of abuse; now it is the Asians and the British. The economic factor is strong in both cases, and General Amin obviously looks on the 60,000 Asians in Uganda much as Hitler looked on the Jews: one believes, as the other did before, that the economy in particular and society in general will not be healthy until they are got rid of. The stranglehold of Belgian big business in the Congo produced much the same reaction from Patrice Lumumba and his successors (excluding Tshombe). But whereas the Congolese

Army's hatred of the white man was largely understandable (after all they still had Belgian officers at Independence, and the mercenaries were white) in Uganda it is something that has been deliberately whipped up by General Amin for no reason except that he has been savaged in the British press. It is hard to know if he is mentally unstable, or whether he is simply brutal and reckless, liable to kill someone at the smallest whim. I believe the latter. His behaviour calls to mind the incident at the Ethiopian court when the explorer Burton presented a hunting rifle. The emperor lifted it up and shot one of his pages. Everyone exclaimed at the efficacy of the weapon, no one was a bit worried about the boy.

Amin will have his way. He will get rid of the Asians, and get his hands on their property, just as the Congolese did when the Belgians took to their heels. Responsible Asians I spoke to left me in no doubt that not a single Asian wants to stay on in Uganda, and even if Amin compels some of the teachers, doctors and technicians to stay for a while, by denying them exit permits, they will leave sooner or later.

If Amin carries out his threat to put those who do not leave by the deadline of November 7 in camps under military guard the situation could become extremely dangerous, and the exodus of the 7,000 British, some of them in remote spots upcountry, must become a very strong possibility. Already schools and hospitals are seriously affected by loss of staff, and with the departure of the Asians, economic chaos and collapse must follow. All this, it could be said, happened in the Congo yet the Congo is still functioning today. But there was one very big difference. The United Nations force in the Congo, with all its faults, did keep the country on its feet, just managing to stagger along.

But who will do this for Uganda? Not the UN. Not the British. Not Jomo Kenyatta or Julius Nyerere. And as for Libya, Colonel Gaddafi may have sent some troops, but the loan of £10 million he is said to have promised General Amin, has, by all accounts, never materialised. Uganda is broke, due largely to over-spending on the Army. Of the Africans who take over the Asian businesses, 90 per cent are expected to go bankrupt. And it is then, the Asians say, that they will be accused of economic sabotage, those who have been unlucky enough not to get out. All this may not happen until the end of the year, but it seems an inexorable process. The Congo, of course, survived because it is one of the richest countries in Africa, as well as one of the biggest; a major world producer of copper and industrial diamonds. Uganda is small and although it produces coffee and tea, it is not in the same league.

At the moment General Amin's Kakwa bully boys, whose tender mercies I personally experienced, are bashing their African opponents, tribal, religious and political. Obote and his exiled army, probably less than a thousand strong, seem to have been destroyed as a fighting force. The Army has already been purged of opponents and potential opponents. The Catholic Baganda, although the largest tribe in Uganda, are cowed and powerless. Uganda is small enough for Amin to exercise almost complete control – provided he has the Army behind him. What happens when there are problems of paying the troops is another matter when the Asians have all been looted, and their cars confiscated. Of course there is always Colonel Gaddafi, and General Amin did have the richest man in East Africa, Manubhai Madvany, whose interests range from steel to matches, behind bars in the notorious Makindye Barracks. And he can always put him back again if he wants to put the squeeze on him.

Much ridicule used to be directed at the United Nations force in the Congo. But I am sure there are a lot of frightened people in Kampala these days who would give a lot to see a pair of Swedish Bluebells go by, or a jeep patrol of Nigerians: in fact anyone at all who looked calm and responsible.

The press had a difficult and sometimes dangerous time in the Congo. A few journalists lost their lives. But, perhaps because you could usually hitch a ride, so to speak, with the mercenaries, or the UN or the Katangese even, there was some protective colouring available. But in Uganda, the press will face an even grimmer test. It may be possible for the agencies and one or two newspapers to keep correspondents sitting tight and filing government handouts, or at most, very guarded interpretations of events. But actually to go and see what is happening for oneself, which is the essence of good reporting, would seem at the moment at any rate to be impossible. And after all that has happened in the past few weeks, it would be a rash man who tried it.

Spectator, 18 November 1972   *Robert Conquest*

FREEDOM OF SCREECH

I lately came across a truly dreadful example of the way in which students are encouraged to violate the rights of others and the decencies of society. Specifically, this was an expression, by the Rector of Dundee, of the view that 'freedom of speech' is compatible with the forcible prevention of speech unpalatable to the left. Such a line is common enough in America, and in France and Germany too, but is usually put under a heavy disguise of incomprehensible syntax and meaningless or ambiguous polysyllables. This time it is a British phenomenon expressed in simple and shameless phrasing.

The passage I am referring to is an interview (in the *Boston Globe*, June 18, 1972) given by Mr Peter Ustinov. In it he describes his duties as Rector of the University of Dundee. Possibly he has been misreported, or partly misreported. One hopes so. At any rate, what he is given as saying in direct speech, surrounded by inverted commas, is the following:

I have a kind of ombudsman role, I'm supposed to speak up on behalf of students. For example, I arrived in the middle of a 'free speech' issue on campus. Enoch Powell, Conservative Member of Parliament, who I suppose is our Agnew figure in England, had been invited by Conservatives to speak at the University. I found 'Powell Go Home' signs painted on the walls. I eventually spoke with detectives and policemen and said it should be brought home to Powell that he would not be safe. They said with normal craft pride, as the psychiatrists call it, that he would be well protected. I asked whether they could also guarantee the safety of the students. They said they couldn't. I then pointed out that Mr Powell would be there for one afternoon. He would make exactly the same speech he'd made everywhere else; whereas the students would be there for another three years and it would be tragic if some students got expelled or hurt simply because the police were protecting Mr Powell. They found the point well taken and Mr Powell was dissuaded from coming. I was attacked and accused of gagging free speech. I said I didn't think this was true. We all know what Powell is going to say in advance, and whatever he says is given broad publicity, it doesn't matter whether he says it on campus or elsewhere.

What could be plainer than that? From it we draw certain clear conclusions. First, if one knows, or thinks one knows, what a speaker will say, then he has no right to say it. As a matter of fact, Mr Enoch Powell (with whom I for one am, incidentally, seldom in agreement) is well known for having a variety of themes and for producing striking surprises in his speeches. But even if this were not so, it would be a curious doctrine to interpret 'freedom of speech' as 'freedom only to say what you have not said before'. One wonders, too, whether the same principle would be applied to, say, Mr Frank Allaun or Miss Bernadette Devlin, who are at least equally – and many would say rather more – susceptible to the charge that one knows what they are going to say. Somehow, one has the feeling that what would apply here is that central slogan of leftiness, 'It's all right when *we* do it.'

Secondly, we now learn that if it would be possible for a speaker to speak elsewhere, he can legitimately be stopped speaking in the place he wants to speak in. This is a principle that could be extended. For example, a landlady or a club would be entitled to refuse a coloured applicant, so long as there were other places where he could get in, and this would constitute no encroachment on his freedom. Or if not, why not?

In the particular circumstances at the university at which Mr Ustinov rectorises, we are also on interesting ground. In part, this is agreeably farcical, as when students are likely to be 'expelled or hurt simply because the police were protecting Mr Powell.' Something seems to be missing from this picture.

So, too, the idea of the police being unable to guarantee the safety of the students as well as of Mr Powell is a sad one. It may perhaps remind one, in a way, of the failure of the British anti-aircraft batterces protecting London to guarantee the safety of the Luftwaffe pilots.

But there are further points to be made. Mr Ustinov represents himself as speaking up 'on behalf of students.' But it was a student society which invited Mr Powell. Mr Ustinov did not speak up on their behalf. As representative of the students, in fact, he saw his role as representing one faction of them, not all of them – indeed, on a literal reading, as representing students (or possibly others) whom he had not seen: those who had painted up 'Powell Go Home!' We ought to be able to assume that if other students (or non-students) had painted up 'Ustinov Go Home,' he would instantly have left. But I do not think we can.

More seriously, one complains less of the disgraceful muddle-headedness, the intellectual corruption, the anti-libertarian prejudice than of the pandering to precisely the lowest and most anti-educational attitudes of certain students. First, it is represented as a 'tragedy' if students are penalised for assault. That is, they are encouraged to regard themselves as infants whose tantrums will not be held against them. They are pampered, in fact, in the most regressive and childlike attitudes and granted exemption from the adult world. But the process of education is in part a process of maturing. It is not a 'tragedy' if students – or anyone else – are held responsible for their actions, it is a condition of civic society.

All in all, Mr Ustinov is encouraging thuggery. But worse still, he is a sponsor, or at least an accomplice, in teaching students a Newspeak attitude – which is to say that he is actively assisting in the process of diseducation. One would prefer totalitarian, or semi-totalitarian, views not to be taught; but if they are, even they should at least be taught at an intellectual level higher than this naïve collection of untruisms.

New Statesman, 19 January 1973   William Shawcross
THE TYRANT IN THE WHITE HOUSE

This Friday evening, if the members of the Philadelphia Orchestra ignore appeals that they protest against the B-52 bombing of Hanoi, President Nixon, hands as usual folded piously in his lap, will enjoy their playing music of his own choice at his Inauguration concert. That choice includes a medley of American patriotic songs and the *1812* overture. There will be four cannon ('simulated B-52s', complains one violinist who feels that the musicians are being asked to 'be good Germans') to help the orchestra crash out Tchaikovsky's triumphant shout of victory and vindication.

He just adores that tune at any time but how very, very appropriate it is this weekend as he embarks on his final four years of power and well, yes, why not – glory. Given his 'success' in Vietnam, Tchaikovsky's sentiment could hardly be more apt. For doesn't he have good reason to feel victorious and vindicated? Isn't his B-52-ing of Hanoi already obviously justified? Who is to deny that the apparent progress made in the peace talks these last 10 days is the direct result of 'Operation Rolling Santa' (as some cynics saw fit to call it). Nobody, and certainly not Olof Palme, can say that the North Vietnamese would have come to their senses if another 5,000 of their civilians hadn't been killed and wounded, 16,000 of their homes destroyed. And having shown his courage in the face of world opinion last month is he not now displaying spectacular magnanimity by stopping all the bombing of North Vietnam? And is peace not now almost clutched between his fingers? No, of course the Inauguration has nothing to do with the timing of this latest flurry of 'hopes' – it is the future of the Vietnamese people he has been concerned with all along – not any dates so petty as elections or inaugurations. Still, just think how spectacular it will be if Henry can ride down Constitution Avenue on an inaugural float tomorrow, bowing and waving and grinning madly and pulling peace (tied to his wrist) squealing from a hat. (Metaphorically speaking, of course, for no one in this Administration, not even Henry, behaves like that.)

The Inauguration celebrations will almost be Nixon's first public appearance since the election. Much of the last two months he has spent in seclusion in the presidential retreat of Camp David, perched on top of a hill in Maryland. He uses Camp David far more than any other president because, he says, 'I find that here on top of the mountain it is easier for me ... to get a proper perspective.' There is a good case, however, for saying that his mountain sojourn is in fact seriously impairing his judgement and convincing him that his election victory has made of him a latter-day plastic Zeus who can play the world from above, disdaining life and opinion, casting thunderbolts down upon those mere mortals who dare even to question his plans for them.

Nixon was never a man remarkable for warmth, humility, sincerity, humanity or a modest sense of his own shortcomings. But now, his last election won, he appears suddenly more aloof, more grandiose, more arrogant, more megalomaniac even, than ever. Swathed in a cloak of contempt – for the media, for Congress, for world opinion and even for the American people itself – he seems to be stripping off the guileful but restricting mask of politician in which we all came to know and love him, to reveal beneath the granite features of a man dedicated to absolute rule. It is cause for some alarm.

His aides make much of his overwhelming victory in November. They ignore the fact that in congressional terms the election was a victory for the Democrats and that the people seemed thus to be voting against McGovern rather than for Nixon or his Republicans. They ignore it completely. On his bombing of Hanoi, on his withholding funds authorised by Congress for social programmes, on his arbitrary reorganisation of government, on his curbs upon the media ... and over, and over again we hear the White House janissaries repeating their self-serving liturgy: 'The President has a mandate, the President has a mandate ...' That this is quite untrue is all to the good. For it demonstrates more clearly the enormity of his power.

When Nixon was still a politician he used sometimes to worry about the media, about Congress and especially about the people. As late as last October he was saying that if a president 'finds that the course he has to take is not popular, he has to explain it to the American people and gain their support.' Not now he doesn't. Nixon has made no attempt whatsoever to explain the bombing either to the people or to Congress. He no longer considers it necessary to win their support. He has given no press conference since early November and, although he claims to be a Disraeli conservative, his contemptuous dealing with the legislature is more reminiscent of De Gaulle. Under extreme pressure he eventually invited a group of congressional leaders to breakfast 10 days ago, curtly told them just what he wanted to say on Vietnam and then, refusing all questions, strode out of the room, leaving them alone with their grapefruit and their ignorance.

For no other reason than to show Congress his disregard of its status, he has declined to follow the example followed by every president since Wilson (including Nixon, the politician, in 1969) and deliver the State of the Union address in person. Instead it will be sent along to Capitol Hill in an envelope. As he seeks to diminish the legislature, so is Nixon trying (successfully) to exalt the executive. At the beginning of his first term Nixon gave each cabinet member supreme authority in his department, allowing him to hire, fire and run it as he chose. At cabinet meetings each member was the spokesman of his department. Nixon the politician then believed in the espousal and interchange of ideas. Nixon the ruler does not.

He has now created three new super bureaucracies (against congressional wishes) for home affairs. They will be controlled by men answerable to him, not to Congress. The idea of independent departmental heads has vanished. There is now no one to plead for housing, for the environment, no one to do any special pleading at all – least of all for health or welfare. Nixon is in fact cutting right back on many of the country's health and social security programmes in the contemptuous belief that 'the average American is like a child . . . if you pamper him and cater to him too much you are going to make him a soft, spoiled and eventually very weak individual.' There's no place for a Pat Moynihan-type welfare reform in this Administration.

For all his promises to bring government closer to the people, Nixon is in fact making it more remote than ever. From now on, decisions will be taken by a small, almost unknown, group of very hard men in the White House, men whom Congress cannot summon for questioning, men who are responsible to no one but Nixon and who are expected to do for home affairs what Kissinger tried to do for the world. This is the more alarming because these 'cowboys' are men of even less quality than Kissinger himself. Men like John Ehrlichman and Robert Haldeman, they have been chosen because of their long record of humourless and unquestioning loyalty to Nixon, not, like Kissinger, because of any outside reputation of worth.

Indeed, many of those nominees to come from outside are distinguished by nothing so much as their sleaziness. Pat Brennan, the new Labour Secretary, ran the New York Construction workers, one of the more corrupt and racist unions in the country; the new head of the Office of Manpower and Budget (which by-passes the Treasury) is Roy Ash, who comes from Litton Industries, a firm currently being accused by Congress of defrauding the government on naval contracts. Men like these and scandals such as the Soviet wheat deal and the Watergate break-in (the Watergate trial is now under way but the defendants have almost all been induced to plead guilty so as to avoid the risk of cross-questions incriminating anyone close to Nixon) all lend the

Administration a nauseous flavour of piety, corruption and bullying.

When a top civil servant told a Senate committee that Eisenhower – who had also encountered Ash's generosity with public money – 'must be twitching in his grave' at the appointment, his resignation was immediately demanded. When he refused to resign he was transferred to upgrade the curriculum at the naval school in Annacostia – the equivalent of exile to Siberia. Back in the Fifties Nixon the politician had campaigned to allow civil servants freedom to make just such criticisms. But not of Nixon the ruler, of course, for he, apostle of anti-care, lamb of Billy Graham, bomber of Hanoi, was elected 'with an overwhelming mandate' and is therefore right, as well as free, to do as he chooses.

Nixon's special contempt is reserved for the media. Although he says he never reads the papers or watches television and looks only at a special news digest prepared each morning by his staff, he seems determined to restrict, harass and if possible tether the press, perhaps because of his fury that journalists do not understand, as he does, that 'when a president has to make a hard decision he has the right to expect support from the so-called opinion leaders . . . who have the educational background to understand the importance of standing behind the president.'

He is no longer prepared to reason with those who do not joyfully cry 'my President right or wrong' and the Administration, infuriated by the *Washington Post*'s brilliant investigations of the Watergate scandal, is trying to create an atmosphere of fear and uncertainty which will inhibit the media's coverage of government affairs. (An example of Nixon's spitefulness is that to punish the *Post*, its White House social correspondent, an inoffensive woman of over 60, is, for the first time in her life, banned from many of them now.) The news networks have been accused of 'ideological plugola' and the government has proposed new regulations which will force local TV stations to censor network programmes, or risk their licences. Following a decision by Nixon's new Supreme Court, serious investigative journalists are now being harassed to reveal their sources whenever a grand jury requires it. In the last weeks several journalists have been imprisoned for refusal; hundreds more are prepared to face imprisonment but nearly all are finding, as the Administration hoped they would find, that their sources are drying up for fear that when the crunch comes the reporters will not in fact choose martyrdom but will tell.

To many people Nixon has always seemed unsympathetic. Not a few more, all around the world, were convinced by his B-52-ing of Hanoi that he is also a spiteful, malignant and dangerous man. Until now he had usually tried, not always successfully, to conceal that malignancy under various political veneers. Now he no longer worries because he is no longer a politician. He is, in effect, the most powerful government in the world. It is early days yet, but it does seem that he means to try to force on America and the rest of us a great deal of his own special philosophy of life.

That will be extremely unpleasant. Judging by his behaviour since November, Nixon's philosophy is now one in which arrogance becomes criminal thuggery, scorn becomes contempt and contempt hatred; it is a philosophy of revenge in which anger turns to vicious spite, in which charity, tolerance and humility are usurped by sanctimony; it is one in which 'nice guys' have no place because 'nice guys don't win ball games', and only winning matters; in which money, however it is obtained, speaks louder than words, and the President doesn't speak at all except to those who adore him. It was summed up most accurately (if in terms which Nixon, we are told, does not ever employ) by his former aide, Charles Colson, when he said at a White House meeting: 'Bugger their hearts and minds, just grab 'em by the balls for Crissake.' And if they still don't do as they're told then bomb their hospitals if they're gooks, and if they're not, well, snatch away their crutches, end their social security payments, close down their TV stations, lock up their reporters, bug their offices, interfere with their courts and snaffle their representatives. But hurry, man, hurry – don't waste time telling them why it's happening to them – they'll come to their senses and understand in the end. Just like Hanoi did – and, anyway, history will prove me right. Now just let's hear the *1812* once again and then it's back up the mountain for a bit more 'perspective' – Billy Graham's coming up to pray.

New Statesman, 16 March 1973   *John Coleman*
STICK MAN

Last Tango in Paris *Prince Charles*

Some men – and women – are born voyeurs, some achieve voyeurism, and some have voyeurism thrust upon them. Let me expose a private part or two. As a professional eavesdropper, almost daily invited to feast my eyes on more screened human flesh than a full-time squad of Casanovas or Catherine the Greats could handle, I am slowly but surely acquiring a resistance to others in (or apparently in) the old act, which expresses itself (or rather doesn't express itself) in my body. How germane this confession may prove as a contribution to the great censorship debate I'm uncertain, but I thought Mrs Whitehouse might like to know. No danger of this column rushing rampant from the cinema in search of satisfaction. More to the point is its relevance to Bernardo Bertolucci's *Last Tango*, comprehensively canvassed as the most something or other yet. Pauline Kael, for instance has dipped heavily into her sack of superlatives: 'This must be the most powerfully erotic movie ever made, and it may turn out to be the most liberating.' And here is Robert Altman, a sometimes splendid director: 'Bertolucci has carried film honesty to its ultimate. It is a standard for looking at films of the past and judging films of the future.' Now experience teaches that it is unlikely any contemporary work of art can live with such praise and one was prepared to make allowances. Nothing prepared me, however, for the stretches of ennui and embarrassment to come.

The immediate cause for embarrassment is Marlon Brando. For reasons best known to himself, he has elected to shamble and strut about in a part that gives full rein to his Method and some to his madness. It is rather as if he had thrown over his once-capable shoulders a quilt tacked together at random from scraps of his old movies and even, alarming thought, of his past life. He is Paul, 45-year-old American in Paris; his wife, who ran a seedy hotel and kept him, has just killed herself with a razor; his only present certainty is that he is, in his own words, 'a good stick man'. This last he proceeds to confirm on the deliciously willing person of Jeanne (Maria Schneider), a 20-year-old Montparnassienne, whom he follows into a flat-to-let in Passy and rapidly mounts against a wall. Writing for the NS from Paris on 2 February, David Leitch stole a bolt or two of my thunder (he's absolutely right: on the male side, you never see anything more arousing than Brando's arse), but I must admit there was nothing to set me against the film so far. Bertolucci's basic notion – of a desperate man and complaisant girl chucking all restraint to the winds for a three-day sex-binge – is sound enough and its pursuit afforded plenty of interesting possibilities. Yet, in retrospect, there were warning signs. Those Francis Bacons sharing the credits, for example (distorted portraits of a man and a woman), found swift visual echoes in images through frosted glass: already a kind of borrowed chic was in action. For all the much-vaunted 'honesty', this was to be an *art* film, with a muted palette for those abandoned, animal interiors – reds, ochres, yellows predominating – and a peculiarly arid way of arranging those obsessed limbs.

As for Brando's muted palate (to hear him mumble such key-lines as 'everything outside this place is bullshit' was to remember *Streetcar*), it was simply a distraction. And the longer the piece proceeds, the more of a worry his performance becomes. Men come from nowhere, certainly, and do their doomed or dastardly things before disappearing, but this Paul is endowed with an unhelpful quantity of past, as his rambling monologues ensure. Drunken farming parents, a bit of boxing and bongo-drumming, a time in Tahiti: even Henry Miller's vagrancies make more sense. Jeanne's background has a tremendous likelihood beside it: dead Army father, racist nurse, a TV-producer boy-friend (Jean-Pierre Léaud with his affectations severely curtailed) who is making a Warhol-type documentary on her and proposes marriage.

What in the last resort, and Paris is not yet that, makes me dislike this film so much is the overpowering sense of missed opportunity, of wholesale botching. To read the publicity that has attached itself to *Last Tango* as to a fly-paper is to get the impression of a raw and steadfast look at the essence of pornography. Perhaps I should have gone over the details of the sex-acts – that first quick take, the butter-buggery bit which retains its trousered sadism for all the 10 seconds Mr Murphy saw fit to excise, the desperate masturbation near the end, in that dance-hall where perky tangoists revolve in competition and Paul and Jeanne sit drunken amid a debris of chairs. It is on items like this that the Festival of Light brigade will be training their binoculars, after all. But, in all honesty, my honesty, you would do best to witness these *morceaux choisis* yourselves. I am not unshockable: it is just that other things shock me, not the way of a man with a woman and vice versa. Frankly, I respect Bertolucci as a rare talent in the cinema and there are a few places here where that respect seems justified. Even a time out of time, which is what he must have been after, will have its humorous moments, and some improvisation while Paul is shaving, a later extravagance with a dead rat, a weird interlude during which Paul and his dead wife's lover chat in identical dressing-gowns, all subserve a film that might have been. In its stead, there is a powdered Brando emoting crudely beside his flighty wife's corpse, another dreary monologue with Brando relinquishing his harmonica to talk of the spit hanging from an old man's unlit pipe, a conclusion so melodramatic as to make the dying man's scrupulous parking of his gum on a balcony seem normal.

THE SECOND PREMIERSHIP

Spectator, 9 March 1974   *Unsigned*
EXIT THE SQUATTER

The squatter in No. 10 Downing Street has at last departed. Nothing became his leadership of the nation so ill as the manner of his leaving it. And there is yet one further step to be taken in his humiliation: he must now resign the leadership of the Conservative Party. Mr Edward Heath's monomania was never more clearly seen than in the days after the general election when, a ludicrous and broken figure, he clung with grubby fingers to the crumbling precipice of his power. True, it is said that his first instinct was to resign, and that he was dissuaded from doing so only by the united appeal of his colleagues. But there is no sign that the plea of Mr Whitelaw was more than formal; and Mr Heath was undoubtedly pathetically eager to listen to the specious arithmetic of Lord Carrington and other members of his Praetorian Guard, according to which the Tories, having gained more votes than Labour, though fewer seats, were entitled to continue in office.

This was a more than ordinarily dishonourable and disgusting argument, coming from a party which took office in 1951 on a minority of the popular vote, and from a Prime Minister who has steadfastly, and in direct denial of a solemn undertaking, refused to allow the people to choose between their independence and the disastrous European future he planned for them. And it was particularly dishonourable coming from a Conservative government, which, having entered upon its term with high and reforming hopes, and having betrayed or reversed practically every one of its major policies, was seen to be seeking, with the aid of the Liberals, to cling, not so much to power, for they had little of that left, as to office alone. The spectacle was ludicrous; it was pathetic; it was contemptible. And Mr Heath having been over the weekend a squalid nuisance, remains, as leader of the Tory Party, just that.

The Spectator has sometimes been accused of a vindictive and personal dislike of Mr Heath. The accusation is unfair: for a long time we supported him in practically every one of his policies, save the European. We rejoiced in his 1970 victory, and applauded the determination with which he set about his quiet revolution. Only over the last two years, when policy after policy was reversed, and disastrous alternatives were introduced with an impenetrable blend of self-righteousness and bullying, did we begin to realise how destructive he is for the party as leader, as he has been for the country as Prime Minister. It is not too much to say that Mr Heath has spent nine years trying to ruin the Conservative Party, and three and a half trying to ruin the country. It may seem unfair and unkindly to pursue this line of argument when Mr Heath has resigned. It is not, because he still has, as leader of the main Opposition party, great potential for damaging the interests of that party and the country.

It is necessary only to look at his record. He has, by his European policy, sundered the deep and abiding association in people's minds between the Tory Party and patriotism, an association that has served the party so well. He has, by the sheer incompetence of his handling of governmental affairs, destroyed the conviction that Conservatives are at least moderately efficient in government: it was chilling to Tory ears to hear Mr Wilson, during the campaign, explain almost wearily how Labour were coming in to clear up yet another Tory mess. He has, first, allowed the party to develop an economic policy of free enterprise on which they were elected but in which he merely pretended to believe and, second, demanded the utter reversal of that policy, asking the while from his followers an unexampled subservience which few, knowing the vindictiveness of his unforgiving nature, had the courage to deny him. To cap all this he went to the country on a spurious and fraudulent issue, attempting to incite the people on a law and order issue where no law had been broken, and raising a communist spectre where none existed. Well did Mr Wilson say that Mr Heath was the first British politician to make the British Communist Party seem important: the proof, indeed, of Mr Heath's inadequacy, incompetence and bloody-minded misjudgement came when, in a general election which saw a massive swing away from him, Mr Jimmy Reid, the most popular Communist candidate imaginable, was obliterated in Central Dunbartonshire.

For these reasons Mr Heath must now depart the Tory leadership as quickly as possible, and before he can do more damage. One need glance only briefly at the terrible spectacle of his leading another campaign against Mr Wilson later this year — and there must surely be another election this year — to see the necessity of that. What would he say? What manifesto could he produce? Would he again have the face to demand a large majority in order to continue strong government? How would his cold and barren nature appear to the reporters assembled each morning at his press conferences, who were very nearly overawed during the late campaign by his ruthless command of effrontery? No: it cannot be, and unless the Tory party has taken leave of its senses, it will not be. The humiliating spectacle at the beginning of the week, when Mr Heath, squatting in No. 10, grovelled at the feet of Mr Thorpe, at whom he had so often and so readily sneered in the past – 'Who's he?' he demanded at one press conference – makes it clear that, if the Conservative party is to regain any respect in the eyes of the nation, any regard for its patriotism, any sense of its own dignity, Heath must go.

New Statesman, 12 April 1974   *Auberon Waugh*
SEX WITH SAUCE

Lovers who can communicate only through the agony column of a newspaper have always touched a chord. The advertisements themselves are so reticent that one longs to learn the full story, even if it is the corny old explanation of a wife sending loving messages to her husband who refuses to talk over his newspaper at breakfast. Now the *Sunday Times* has introduced what can only be seen as a refinement of this art form, where messages of a personal nature which husbands and wives are too shy to discuss together in private can be exchanged publicly in the guise of a general dissertation on sex. The pioneers in this field of human communications are that brave and admirable couple Jill Tweedie and Alan Brien.

When Brien and Tweedie married late last year, *Private Eye* ran a special cut-out wedding supplement decorated with bells and Cupids: *For a few precious moments the cares and worries of crisis-torn Britain were forgotten. Men and women everywhere put aside their differences to share the magic of what they are calling the Wedding of the Century.* Even those who could not share the *Eye*'s euphoria felt a certain quiet satisfaction that such a resolute campaigner for women's rights as Tweedie should have been brought at last to the registry office by such a one as Brien. In the words of St Paul: 'But if they cannot contain let them marry; for it is better to marry than to burn.' (I Corinthians vii 9.) One would be less than human if one failed to wonder how they have made out since.

The answer was given through a brief editorial announcement in last week's *Sunday Times*: 'Jill Tweedie and Alan Brien give their verdict on *The Joy of Sex* as a couple for whom sex is already a joy.' In other words, they are making out very well. So far so good. The book they discuss is a rather depressing sex manual* edited by Dr Alex Comfort and written in the illiterate, folksy style one associates with holiday

The Joy of Sex ed. by Dr Alex Comfort. Quartet Books (£6.50).

camps and *Blue Peter*: 'Sex play with long hair is great because of its texture.' It is full of hints for 'mind-blowing turn-ons' like this suggestion for using your partner's armpit in something called *axillary intercourse*:

Put her left arm round your neck and hold her right hand behind her with your right hand. She will get her sensations from the pressure against her breasts, helped by your big toe pressed to her clitoris if she wants it.

From this treasury of helpful advice, Tweedie and Brien extract whatever seems appropriate to their needs. Thus from Tweedie we hear of a section which 'frowns gently and advisedly on the forward male's "direct grab at the clitoris" and advocates, again advisedly, "a lot more attention being devoted to the breasts than the average man may deem necessary".'

I hope that Brien has received this message loud and clear and we won't have to return to the matter again. Tweedie praises the book because the writers do not 'sternly insist on fore-play', averring that 'females, contrary to today's sexual encyclicals, do not always want to wait for it, and one of the greatest aphrodisiacs – not enough emphasised here – is the overpowering desire of the man to do what he has to do.' The message for Brien may be plain enough, but I think she does Dr Comfort an injustice. This particular propensity is covered in the section called 'Quickies'.

Tweedie's loudest complaint is at first glance an alarming one: 'The only real criticism I have of this book is its under-emphasis on sex in the head – which is where for my money it all starts and very nearly finishes.' In fact, one of the longest and most depressing passages in the book, inelegantly called 'Mouth Music', describes every reasonable aspect of this approach to sex. What else must the unfortunate Brien be expected to start on and nearly finish in order to get Tweedie's money – her ears? But on reflection I see that what she must really be saying is that sex is nicer to think about than actually do. So the final recipe for Sex With Tweedie would seem to be this: in the first place just think about it but, if you must do something, mind what you grab and get it over quickly.

Brien tells us that he likes to wash beforehand but his preference is for something 'dark and strange and frightening and unthinking and incredible'. I don't know how Tweedie measures up to his other demands, but in its *unthinking* aspect this ticket seems the exact opposite to Tweedie's cerebral approach.

None of this explains how two intelligent people like Brien and Tweedie can take a ludicrous book like Alex Comfort's *The Joy of Sex* seriously. The explanation may lie in a particular strain of metropolitan life which is well illustrated in another passage of the book under review. It describes itself as a Gourmet Guide to Lovemaking, elsewhere as a Cordon Bleu Guide, and is full of gastronomic imagery – sections are called *Starters*; *Main Courses*; *Sauces & Pickles* etc. But when our lovers actually get into a restaurant they appear to have very little interest in food:

In a restaurant, in these days of tights, one can surreptitiously remove a shoe and sock, reach over and keep her in almost continuous orgasm with all four hands in view on the table and no sign of contact . . . She has less scope, but can learn to masturbate him with her two big toes.

Yes, yes, but what about the food? Last time I saw Brien was at a *Private Eye* lunch when I am glad to say he managed to keep his big toe to himself. To judge from his later comments in the *Sunday Times* he did not enjoy the meal much, creating little pools of embarrassment all around him by asking people: 'Do you *really* think I'm boring or do you just say you do?' But the chief awkwardness came when a voice – it may have been my own, obviously late in the meal – rose above the others announcing that its owner wouldn't really mind if he never had another orgasm in his life. For the first time in our acquaintance I saw Alan Brien look shocked.

That evening, travelling to Paddington on the Underground, I found myself squeezed with about 200 others into a single carriage: Indians, Pakistanis, Jamaicans, French and English, we could only wiggle our eyebrows to signify our appreciation of each others' unassailable human dignity. Suddenly the true explanation for everything occurred to me.

It is common knowledge among those who spend their time shutting up rats in confined spaces – usually in California or the Soviet Union – that the pets' behaviour follows three patterns: first comes a period of enormously heightened sexual activity brought about by physical proximity; next they lose all sex drive and content themselves with eating each other; finally they relapse into apathy and die of malnutrition.

Spectator, 28 September 1974   *Douglas Jay*
VOTING AGAINST EUROPE

In this election the British people will decide whether or not a
referendum is to be held on the straight issue of staying in the Common
Market or coming out. For the Labour Manifesto includes the clear
undertaking that:

Within twelve months of this Election we will give the British people the final
say, which will be binding on the Government – through the ballot box – on
whether we accept the terms and stay in, or reject the terms and come out.

This choice will prove far more crucial for the long-term future of this
country than all the current conventional verbiage about what is mis-
called 'inflation'. Some sceptics may still perhaps wonder why the
phrase 'ballot box' and not 'referendum' appears in the Manifesto. They
should ask themselves whether a Labour Prime Minister with a
majority would wish to hold a third Election 'within twelve months'
rather than a referendum; and their doubts will be dispelled. What is
needed now is an assurance that, as in Elections, fair treatment at the
time of the referendum will be given to the main point of view in the
broadcasting media and that their expenditure will be similarly limited.

It is a great victory for the spirit of our Constitution that the case for
the referendum on this unique issue is now almost universally accepted
only four years after some of us first urged it in the summer of 1970.
The case rests on the basic truth, recognised in nearly all modern
democracies, that the Constitution itself can be altered only by the
people and not by Parliament alone.

This represents the genuine voice of classic British liberalism; and it
can be instructively compared with the Brussels spirit, as enunciated by
M. Jean Rey, ex-President of the EEC Commission, on July 17 in
London: 'A referendum on this matter,' M. Rey said, 'consists of
consulting people who don't know the problems instead of consulting
people who know them. I would deplore a situation in which the policy
of this great country' (Britain) 'should be left to housewives. It should be
decided instead by trained and informed people.'

In deciding whether to vote in this Election for a referendum on the
EEC the public would be wise, first and foremost, to compare the
promises made by pro-Marketeers in 1971 and 1972 with the actual
results of membership. The contrast is indeed staggering. We were

promised – notably in Mr Heath's notorious 1971 White Paper – that economically the 'great market of 250 millions' would soon solve all our economic problems, and that politically there would be 'no erosion of essential national sovereignty.'

And what has happened? In 1974, the second year of membership the UK (which had a payments surplus of £1,000 millions a year in 1971–2) is now running a non-oil deficit of at least £2,000 millions a year; food prices have risen over 50 per cent; and the visible trade deficit with the rest of the EEC (the 'great home market') is itself running at £2,000 millions a year. The latter is perhaps the most glaring of all Mr Heath's deceptions; for his 1971 White Paper said specifically: 'the Government are confident' that the balance with the Six 'will be positive and substantial.' Yet this £2,000 millions is ten times our deficit with the Six before we joined; and actually exceeds our total non-oil deficit with all countries in 1974.

The public, having been grossly misled by the pro-Marketeers in this way, are unlikely to believe them when they now say: 'Well it has all turned out very badly, but it is nothing to do with Market membership.' Unhappily, however, this is not what we were promised in 1971. We were not promised that the Market would only do us moderate damage. We were promised by everyone from Ted Heath to Roy Jenkins that the economic gains would be so great as to justify sacrifice of our political independence as a nation.

Unhappily also for the pro-Marketeers' new myth, the EFTA nations which stayed out are prospering gaily in the alleged desperate world condition of 1974. Norway – whose people were told that 'exclusion' would ruin them – is enjoying the greatest boom in her history, has raised the exchange value of her currency twice in eighteen months, and holds record currency reserves today. And if that is supposed to be all due to the prospect of oil riches; why does not the same prospect have the same effect in Britain?

In the crucial case of food, as well as the trade balance generally, it is clear that membership has already seriously damaged both our living standards and our balance of payments. The Marketeers are now busy in inventing another new myth; that food is cheaper and will remain so in the EEC than outside. If so why is the vast bureaucratic apparatus of the CAP with its import taxes, levies, import bans and 'intervention' hoards needed to prevent food being imported from outside the ring?

The now notorious case of beef is enough to demolish this particular myth. At the moment, all imports of beef from any country in the world into the EEC are totally banned by the Brussels bureaucracy, contrary to GATT principles and in face of angry protests from Australia, New

Zealand, Argentina, Brazil, Yugoslavia, Hungary, Poland and Rumania – all of whom could send us cheaper beef. Meanwhile the marketeers' own beef mountain – too dear for us members to buy – is now over 200,000 tons; and 8,000 tons of it is stored in ships in Bantry Bay because the warehouses are full. But 30,000 has been sold cheap to the Russians again, and is on offer at subsidised low prices to anybody lucky enough not to be an EEC member!

In Britain, not merely are consumers as well as Commonwealth suppliers damaged by the CAP, but our own farmers are hit also. We have been forced to abandon the system of guaranteed prices and deficiency payments which served consumers and farmers so well for twenty-five years and have thus gratuitously created a farming crisis as well. We have needlessly introduced into this country the political clash between farmers and consumers which has long haunted Continental politics.

As a 'Common agricultural market' the CAP is a fiction. But insofar as it is real – the import levies, bans, 'mountains' and so on – it is damaging to Britain.

In the longer term the damage is bound to be greater. For though internal subsidies may keep retail prices down, they cannot alter the terms of trade, and as the commodity price cycle swings again downwards, basic production costs must re-assert themselves. And for almost all staple foods, whatever current prices, *costs of production* are much lower for physical and climatic reasons in Australia, New Zealand, North and South America than on the European Continent. It is fascinating that M. Lardinois, the CAP super-bureaucrat, objected to Britain buying Australian sugar on these long-term grounds. As the *Financial Times* said (September 19): 'The problem with the Australian deal seems to be that there would be no import levy on this specially contracted sugar even if world market prices should drop from their present heights to below EEC levels.' It is *cheaper* Australian sugar that M. Lardinois both fears and expects.

So with the other Great Lie of the 1971 White Paper: 'No erosion of essential national sovereignty.' M. Lardinois's comment on that is as follows: 'From March 1 Britain is no longer free to do as she likes with sugar. On that date the Commonwealth Sugar Agreement will expire, and the Community is taking over responsibility for British supplies.' The ban on beef imports into this country was imposed without debate, let alone approval, by the British Parliament, or even any previous notice to the Commons Scrutiny Committee. Dozens of 'laws' are now being 'adopted' in Brussels every month, claiming enforcement in the British Courts, which have never been discussed by Ministers, let alone any elected body, but purely by officials or 'permanent representatives' (Ambassadors).

Let every British voter on October 10 therefore consider this. Enormous harm has been done to this country by the European Movement. Not merely has our economic strength been grievously weakened, and our best friends alienated; but our unity of purpose in foreign policy has been undermined. Our future in the post-war world depended on our visibly championing the causes of Parliamentary Government, liberal trade policies, social justice and civil liberty; and working closely with our natural partners in the Commonwealth, North America and Northern Europe. Our present hesitations and difficulties are largely due to our having been diverted by the Euro-fanatics from seizing this precious opportunity.

But great as is the damage, the choice is still open: on the one hand to be entangled, like a fly in a cobweb, as one State in a plutocratic Little-Europe Federation, with Germany as the inevitable senior partner; or on the other to regain our political liberty, to fight the battle for ever freer trading policies throughout the world as a member of a widened European Free Trade Area, forming the link between the Commonwealth, Western Europe and North America. If we take the former narrow road, we shall never recover as a nation. That is why a vote on October 10 for an EEC referendum will be decisive for our whole national future, and for much else as well.

New Statesman, 22 November 1974   *Clive James*
SUPPLIER OF POETRY

A Nip in the Air by JOHN BETJEMAN *Murray* £1.50

Collections of John Betjeman's verse don't change, they merely become more appropriate. Betjeman poems have always watched the old England die, the self age, believed fearlessly in the gentle virtues and tremulously in salvation. Neither his earlier nor his later work has required to be falsified in order to achieve such remarkable consistency. Betjeman was simply born old, thereby ruling out the prospect of immaturity; or else is still infantile, with maturity never to arrive; or perhaps both. The co-existence of sage and toddler keeps predictability at bay. The only risk he has run as an artist is of being repetitive.

Everything in *A Nip in the Air* has occurred before. But still the

ambiguities linger, making the best loved and most cuddly of Poets
Laureate a permanent odd-ball. Familiarity is deceptive, although very
familiar. Really he was already By Appointment in the Thirties, as in
'Death of King George V' from *Continual Dew*:

> Spirits of well-shot woodcock, partridge, snipe
> Flutter and bear him up the Norfolk sky . . .

While Edward landed hatless from the air on the runway hemmed in
by a new suburb. Material change threatened the fruitful continuities.
The voice of the old middle class was calling on the aristocracy to
conserve its ways, and still is: the poems to Charles and Anne in this
volume were written by a born monarchist, not a convért. The
disappearing social order whose details he so lovingly records was the
only certain good. Modernism holds no place for his kind. It would be –
well, it is – a message acceptable to any thinking Tory. Opportunistic
rapacity has done for the old order. But it is only lately, at the eleventh
hour, that Betjeman has begun to examine the possibility of the old
middle class and the new rapists being close kin. It would be a
subversive conclusion to most of what he has always said, so it is no
surprise that the conclusion is not quite reached. But 'County' is still an
unusually abrasive effort:

> God save me from the Porkers,
> God save me from their sons
> Their noisy tweedy sisters
> Who follow with the guns . . .

Porker is a *faux-bonhomme* and dull with it, evading taxes while
blasting the pheasants. He is all pedigree and purse (and his womenfolk
are worse). The Porkers set a bad example to the new rich. As the poet
waxes wroth, the reader waxes stunned: it is unusual to find that the
Porkers are not themselves new. For destruction to emanate from
somewhere in the poet's own background is an odd concession from
Betjeman. Perhaps the Porkers, without being really new, are yet
new*ish*. Anyway, the matter is not pursued beyond that, and for most of
the volume the villains are the planners and communicators we have
come to know and loathe.

In 'Executive' the hero is a peach of his genus. Essentially he
integrates, and is basically viable. He does some 'mild developing' on
the side. And Rex, the PRO of 'Shattered Image', is a trapped
paedophile who finds his fellow smoothies dumping him. The new,
usurping middle class doesn't pull together except for advantage.
They find their unity in legalised vandalism, creating nothing but

a wilderness, in which the disinherited working class aimlessly sheds litter. The caravans of the milling plebs jam the shoreline and the wrappings of their potato crisps non-biodegradably choke the surf.

'Let us keep what is left of the London we knew,' Betjeman sighs in 'Meditation on a Constable Picture', but by now he is more resigned than desperate. We remember that in his superlative television programme on Metroland he had already half-waved his goodbye to England. Much of the energy has gone out of his theme: a poignant mark of the enemy's triumph. But for the greater part of his creative life the urge to preserve supplied him with his most important creative impulse. To him and the few writers in his league, the onset of chaos meant the necessity of turning recollection into art. For some time yet it will be an act of critical daring to call Betjeman or Osbert Lancaster anything more lofty than exquisite, but in fact they have transmuted a fleeting reality into a tangible fiction during the moment of its vanishing, and when the vanishing is completed will be easily seen to have performed a service.

Not that they didn't enjoy performing it. The younger Betjeman elegantly lamented an old building even when it was still upright. In 'On Seeing An Old Poet In The Café Royal' from *Old Lights for New Chancels* he wept delightedly for smells gone by – 'Scent of Tutti-Frutti-Sen-Sen/And cheroots upon the floor'. But apart from the lamps, not much about the place had changed. It was just that the people were gone. Betjeman would still have been nostalgic if not a single gasolier had ever been uprooted anywhere in the realm. He is cast back neurotically. His macaronic threnodies, crowded with the names of things remembered, are charms, like the coincidental gatherings of characters in Anthony Powell.

Self-revelation has come slowly in Betjeman's work and there are still many puzzles for those of us not in the know. But in the aggregate of his lyrics – and more clearly than in the avowedly autobiographical *Summoned by Bells* – we can by now clearly see the bitter heritage of his early traumata. Whatever the wounds were, they left him nuzzling his woolly bear for ever, while yearning for that most engulfing of all women, the Betjeman Girl. She survives in this new book as Laurelie Williams, Queen of the Hunt Ball, but her strapping reign of glory started early on. In *Old Lights for New Chancels* she was Pam, the 'great big mountainous sports girl' with the hairy arms, or else Myfanwy, the bikey, dikey Valkyrie, 'chum to the weak'. In *New Bats in Old Belfries* she was Joan Hunter Dunn, the horny-handed tennis-girl of 'A Subaltern's Love-song', who returned, still in those redolent white shorts, as Bonzo Trouncer in *Selected Poems*. In *A Few Late Chrysanthemums* she was equipped with 'the strongest legs in Pontefract' and made yet another appearance as a tennis champ – 'The Olympic Girl' who stared down from a great height and whose racket he would like to have been, so as 'to be press'd/With hard excitement to her breast'. (Of girl cyclists he is on record as desiring to be the saddle.) All this is poised, distanced, suave and funny, but you can see very clearly the regressive hurt.

'You're to be booted. Hold him steady, chaps!' the childhood memory was one of the late chrysanthemums. He was slow to take revenge, never quite realising that it was his class-mates, in both senses, who had a mission to rip up his world. Betjeman puzzled over the inscrutable doings of the *hoi polloi* formiculating in 'the denser suburbs' but never faced the genuine paradox of a civilised order hastening its own ruin. He identified himself with a class at a time when it was not yet fully clear that the class would fail to identify itself with him. They would buy his books while tearing down anything beautiful that stood in their way. Betjeman's audience *are* the developers. He was, from the beginning, in a historical fix. From *Selected Poems* onwards, the apocalypse began to roll in – the sea, which will send its waves for centuries to come, 'when England is not England'.

The sea, 'consolingly disastrous', recurred in his poetry all through the Fifties and is loud in this volume, rustling with campers' jetsam. Betjeman doesn't see a future: he is elegiac to the end of the line – elegiac where his admirer Larkin is tragic, since at least Betjeman is longing for an existence he once led. The past is gone and the future is not worth having – it would be a hell of a message if message were all there was. But the poetry is a cornucopia of cherished things, and the pessimism is all too easily traceable to its author's personality. He fears the loss of his life as he feared the loss of his way of life – he feels unprotected. Death is all through this new book but it was all through the old books too, as vivid as the sadistic threats of his bent nurserymaid. He can be called light-minded only by the thick-witted, and this remains true even though the well-placed find him comforting.

Spectator, 8 February 1975   *Beverley Nichols*

MY RIGHT TO DIE

In March 1974, out of the blue, I had a haemorrhage, and was rushed to hospital for an exploratory operation. This revealed a deep-seated cancer, and two days later there was a further operation, lasting six hours, in which the growth was removed. There followed several weeks in which I hovered between life and death, for, in spite of brilliant surgery and the most devoted nursing, there were 'complications'. But these would make painful reading, so that is all you will wish to be told about my operation, and probably more.

The reason for this article – the first that I have been able to write for nearly a year – is that during these long months of physical torture I have had more than adequate opportunity to check some of my most deeply held convictions concerning the values of life and the values of death, and to reassess them in the light of this experience. Such an examination, if it is honestly conducted, inevitably compels the quester to face the ultimate problem of suicide. This, in its turn, obliges him to make up his mind about voluntary euthanasia – the legalised inducement of death.

And please do not console yourself with the idea that this is an academic problem in which you have no concern. Some 10 per cent of the readers of this article will be obliged to face up to it before they die, either on their own behalf or on behalf of some relation or friend. Why not do so *now*, before pain has deprived them of the power of logical thought?

I imagine that if there were to be a national poll on the pros and cons of suicide, it would produce a result in which the 'don't knows' greatly outnumbered all the rest. If the poll were international the confusion would be even greater. In Japan, in certain circumstances, it is a proof of honour and courage; in India it can be greeted as a pious duty; throughout the realms which obey the doctrines of the Roman Catholic Church, it is a mortal sin. The Protestant churches, apparently, are not so sure. Such a confusion of counsels argues an equal confusion of understanding.

Which side are you on? And why?

To me the whole problem begins and ends with physical pain, and I often suspect that those who are most vehement in their denunciation of voluntary euthanasia have never really experienced pain at all. Not pain with a capital 'P'. They may have had broken arms or fractured wrists, various abscesses, hernias, migraines, shingles, fistulas, kidney stones etc etc – to mention a few of the physical bothers of which I have personal experience – but to describe these as 'pain' is ridiculous. Compared with the pain of certain types of cancer they are minor annoyances.

I have actually *seen* pain, very clearly indeed, at close quarters. You may be interested to learn what it looks like. Pain, pictorially, is a

cluster of serpents in various shades of colour that are essentially evil –
virulent green, arsenic pink, muddy crimson and slimy black. When
they first flash across the vision they are huddled together, at some
distance from the body, in a loathsome cluster, palpitating, watching,
waiting. Then as the crisis mounts, they begin to detach themselves, and
to slide closer and closer, slowly, relentlessly, with a soft, gloating hiss.
And now they are upon their victim, beginning to enter his body, one by
one, gliding up his limbs, flooding him with scalding poison through
their forked tongues, higher and higher, till they reach the brain. This is
the moment when, if one is lucky, one loses consciousness – the
moment when one drifts into a temporary limbo of hell or – if one is
very lucky indeed – into the permanent liberty of death.

But one is not always that lucky. For the serpents of pain are very
cunning creatures – schooled by Nature, the arch-sadist, in every trick
of the torturer's trade. They know precisely when to stop. So they begin
to retreat, slithering downwards, flickering their poisoned tongues,
detaching themselves, withdrawing to the distance, regrouping, waiting,
watching.

And there is a sharp prick in the arm, the sickly reek of ether, and the
nurse gives another injection. Till the next time. That is Pain.

This picture that I have painted is not an airy fantasy; still less is it a
horror comic. It is a factual description by a practised reporter of an
ordeal to which thousands of men and women are subjected, often for
months and sometimes for years, because those who framed our laws
are too blind, too ignorant or too prejudiced to face the facts.

If it is a crime to kill a man, is it not a greater crime to sentence him to
a living death? We did not wish to come into this world, so why should
any man dictate to us how or when we decide to leave it? These are
questions that have never been satisfactorily answered, least of all by
the church.

Sometimes, during the crises of the past year, I have received
religious consolation at the bedside, and it was indeed consolation of a
sort. There is a blessing in the holy sacrament even when you are too
weak to lift the cup that holds the sacred wine. But it does not dispel the
serpents. They lie there coiled, watching, ready to strike again. When
the priest had gone, leaving me alone to await their assaults, I have
wished that he might have stayed a little longer, not only to comfort me
by his presence but to answer the fundamental questions which all
Christians should try to answer, but seldom do. For example . . .

If suicide is to be regarded by the church as a mortal sin, why did
Christ never even bother to mention it? Why was it left to the church to
assume, with no authority whatsoever, that He *would* have condemned

it if anybody had asked Him? The ecclesiastical argument, conveniently ignoring the teaching of the Master – or rather His lack of teaching – is to the effect that it is a mortal sin because it is an affront to God – a wilful rejection of the 'gift of life.'

The 'gift of life'! I have small patience with that phrase. The value of a gift is to be measured by the happiness which it brings to the recipient. I wonder if any of my readers chanced to see a photograph recently reproduced by a scientific journal in America – of a pair of Siamese twins? They were both girls, about two years old, and no operation could be devised to separate them. One of them had been born with a high intelligence but she was gradually losing it because her sister, remorselessly attached to her by chains of flesh, had been born mad. By what possible concept of religion can it be argued that these children should be compelled to endure their tortures to the bitter end?

Here is a very personal confession with a direct bearing on the subject. It was inevitable, during the past year, that I should contemplate suicide, and through the long nights, when the serpents would permit, I lay awake devising schemes which would involve the least difficulty for myself and the least distress for my friends. Some of these schemes had an element of farce. There was one, in particular, which involved going down to Cornwall and driving out to Land's End in the middle of the night. Having arrived I would get out of the car, swallow a handful of pills washed down with a bottle of spirits and struggle into a heavily weighted overcoat. Thus equipped, I would stagger down the cliffs, and totter off a rock into the icy waters.

The trouble was that I did not know what sort of spirits to swallow nor what sort of tablets to take. Then, as though to confirm my resolution, the papers reported the death of Desmond Donnelly, the former MP for Pembroke. He killed himself in a hotel near Heathrow. By his bed was an empty bottle of vodka and an empty bottle of barbiturates. He had taken twenty 200 milligramme tablets of . . . we will call it 'X'. I had a full bottle of this powerful drug in my medicine cupboard at home. So that was that. I knew what had to be done.

But I did not do it, for two reasons. The first was another operation, which left me too weak to make any plans at all. The second was a visit from a very dear friend. We will call him Derek. I had known him for twenty years; we had no secrets from one another; and I told him that I had lost the will to live, and wanted out. He took the news quite calmly. He certainly was not shocked, for he was suffering from an incurable disease of the bones. 'But if you are thinking of suicide,' he said, 'forget it.' Then he told me that a month ago he had tried to kill himself, using precisely the same methods as Donnelly. But something went wrong.

He had taken either too much or too little, and after three days his body dragged him back to life. Six months later he died in hospital after the amputation of his right leg.

I shall always remember his last words, when he left me alone to grapple with the serpents. 'In a civilised society,' he said, 'it would be as easy to buy the ingredients of a suicide, with precise directions, as it is to buy a first aid kit.'

'But if that were possible,' cry the opponents of euthanasia, 'people would be committing suicide for the most trivial reasons – a headache, a row with the wife, a warning letter from the inspector of taxes.' I very much doubt it. The will to live is the most potent force in the heart of man. Only in the absolute extremities of pain is it likely to be surrendered. The purpose of voluntary euthansia is to meet those extremities.

For what they are worth, which is very little, let us consider the moral and practical objections.

The anti-euthanasiasts draw horrifying pictures of the legal abuses which, they claim, would inevitably follow any act empowering the medical profession to ease the last days of the dying. They present us with the prospect of wicked nephews gathering round the bedside of the nearly departed, doing terrible things with last wills and testaments, aided and abetted by evil nurses and unscrupulous doctors. Such fears are ridiculous. The safeguards suggested in the charter of the Voluntary Euthanasia Society which would almost certainly form the basis of any future legislation, are so comprehensive and so stringent that even the wickedest of nephews would find it impossible to get away with any dirty work. He would be checked and counter-checked at every stage of the game.

Moreover the dying man would have the added consolation of knowing that he had disposed of his affairs *in advance*, while his brain was still functioning rationally. One of the greatest horrors of acute pain is that it drives men mad. Quite literally mad. Indeed, the anti-euthanasiasts, by their determination to prolong life at all costs, are actually defending a system whereby it is not only necessary to turn men into lunatics but compulsory to do so.

Perhaps the most illusory argument against legalised euthanasia is the one which claims that it is no longer necessary because of the discovery of so many hypnotics, sedatives, analgesics and tranquillisers, which keep pain within 'tolerable' limits. This is simply not true. How can any narcotic, however potent, make life 'tolerable' for a man who is suffering from an inoperable cancer of the throat, which gradually makes it impossible for him to swallow and after a few weeks makes it almost impossible for him to breathe? And why, since there are so few hospitals for terminal illnesses, should he be condemned to breathe his last in the full publicity of a public ward, which is almost certainly understaffed?

When all other arguments are exposed as false the opponents of legalised euthanasia usually invoke some form of moral code, claiming that it would be against the will of God. It would transgress the sixth commandment; it would violate the principle that 'suffering is God's gift for the good of our souls that we may grow in grace.' The best answer to this pious nonsense was made by the late Dean Inge of St Paul's. 'I cannot believe,' he said, 'that God wills the prolongation of torture for the benefit of the soul of the sufferer.'

There is one – and in my opinion only one – valid argument against the immediate legalisation of voluntary euthanasia with the patient's consent. This is that it might be the means of deterring some patients suffering 'terminal' disease from receiving the benefits of spirit healing. In spite of the massive body of evidence in its favour, the attitude of the majority of doctors towards spirit healing is that it 'can't do any harm', and the majority of patients turn to it as a last resort. The very fact that it *is* so often a 'last resort', the final effort to escape an 'incurable' condition, when all else has failed, gives added weight to the miracles which the healers have accomplished. I use the word 'miracle' advisedly, for it is the word which has constantly been used by doctors, nurses and hospital matrons when confronted by the otherwise inexplicable cures for which the healers have been responsible.

This article could go on for ever, and I need hardly say that I would willingly have forgone the year of torture which has given me the material to write it. But I would like to think that one man's agony and his reactions to it, may help, in however small a measure, to bring comfort to many. As I said before, this is not an academic matter. The serpents of pain are no respectors of persons.

New Statesman, 25 April 1975   *Richard West*

THE SACRIFICE OF SAIGON

A friend and colleague came to my hotel room late the other night and insisted on hearing my views on what he called 'the morality of the Vietnam crisis'. Although whisky fuddled his exposition, I grasped his dilemma: how to reconcile his abstract belief that communism would benefit the mass of Vietnamese with a feeling of pity for the minority who now live in great fear. It is the same argument that was fought between Edmund Burke and Thomas Paine at the start of the French Revolution, an argument of which Paine won the first round with his clever quip that Burke 'pitied the plumage but forgot the dying bird'. It is an argument worth reviving now that 15 North Vietnamese divisions menace Saigon, which has barely seven divisions of disheartened men.

There is no need now to repeat all the rude things that I and others have said in the past about this particular South Vietnamese bird. The horrible aspects of life in Saigon have grown still more horrible in the last month under the influence of fear. A few days ago I heard a girl weeping because her sister, a prostitute, had died of VD at the age of 19 after a night in which she slept with five men. She was one of the hundreds of thousands of drug addicts in Saigon who have grown still more desperate since the heroin ran out and who now have to find £4 or £5 a day to 'shoot up' boiled opium, speed or sleeping pills. In the smart middle-class cafés, just as much as on the pavements around Le Lai, one sees countless young people, army deserters and crippled veterans bearing injection scabs on their wrists or ankles; the limbless 'shoot up' through a vein in the side of the head.

Few of the pox-ridden get penicillin and few addicts are cured by being thrown into prison. At one prison recently, I am told on good authority, a legless addict who had hurled his soup at a warder was tied up by the arms and beaten with his own crutches. An eye-witness described to me how a young man in a drug coma was carried into a hospital, kicked to make sure he was still alive and then placed on a bed with an old man who had been dead three days.

It must be pointed out, however, that the epidemics of VD and drugs are largely attributable not to the Saigon regime but to the Americans who departed two years ago, leaving their grisly souvenirs. When American troops were here in hundreds of thousands, the army doctors gave weekly, preventive injections of anti-biotics to all the girl camp-followers, thus ensuring that they developed immunity to the medicine and never lost the disease. The drug trade was actually run by the CIA, who wanted to please the Highland opium growers, thus making them willing mercenaries.

The bad state of the hospitals is also largely attributable to the Americans and other foreign countries who sent in their own doctors, thus encouraging the Vietnamese doctors to leave for private practice. As an experienced social worker told me this week: 'Between the time when the foreign doctors left and the time when the Vietnamese doctors came back to the hospitals, many thousands of patients died unnecessarily. It was the Americans who created, on principle, an economy and society based on acquisitiveness and selfishness, graced with the slogan "private enterprise".'

One can blame the Americans, but the society they created here that foreigners so smugly condemn is no different in essence from the society that we in Britain have built over the last 20 years. Those British people who read of South Vietnam's corrupt regime might be interested to know that even now in Saigon the public services and the government bodies work more efficiently than in London. The water and electricity boards work with a speed I envy, recalling the long delays that my wife and I suffer in getting someone to empty the gas meter.

It is not true to portray South Vietnam as a fascist regime overthrown by a revolutionary movement. Even at this eleventh hour opposition movements have some right of protest, while Saigon's press is less timid than London's in its exposure of rascals in office. The Vietcong or indigenous southern communists now play only a tiny part in the war; the Saigon proletariat, which ignored two calls for an uprising in 1968, seems more apathetic than revolutionary. What began as guerrilla war has turned into an old-fashioned conventional invasion of the South by the North, which has an immense advantage in tanks, artillery and divisions. We are seeing now something similar to the Korean war, with interesting differences.

In Korea the anti-colonial movement, against the Japanese, had been led by right-wing nationalists, while the communists had been led into the North behind the guns of the Russian army. In Vietnam it was the communists who led the anti-colonial movement so that the nationalists, in order to fight them, were obliged to ally first with the French and then with the Americans. This never meant they were puppets of foreigners. Puppets do not volunteer to parachute to a certain death, as 50 Vietnamese officers volunteered to drop into Dien Bien Phu on the day before it was captured in 1954.

It is distasteful, here in Saigon, to read the gloating tone of some foreign newspapers over the fate of the anti-communists here. Such a tone is acceptable from members of the Communist party (not Trotskyist, whose group here was exterminated by Ho Chi Minh), from those without property, mortgage, or motor-car; from those who do not wish to visit a foreign, non-communist country. The gloating is unacceptable from the rich radical chic who are even now doubtless planning to hire a refugee South Vietnamese au pair girl.

The double-think is especially horrible with regard to the Roman Catholics, who number about 10 per cent of the population and many of whom are refugees from the North, where many of their coreligionists were murdered. Their prospects under communism are, to say the least, less agreeable than those of the Catholics in Ulster who are merely cheated out of a vote or a job at the shipyard. I find it strange that trendy left-wing apologists for the fascist hooligans of the Provisional IRA should express so little concern for Catholics here.

No, I have not forgotten the dying bird, and probably most people here now want the VC to come if only to stop the fighting. My argument is directed not against the communists but against the foreign capitalist powers that provoked and prolonged this war: first the British who came here in 1945 to restore French colonialism (a policy in which they had the surprising support of the NS); then the French who fought here eight years; then the Americans who fought here seven years, with the eager support of Harold Wilson – a puppet if ever there was one. The capitalist powers have abandoned the Vietnamese because they cannot afford them in a recession and a fuel crisis. We, of whatever social class, who enjoy the riches of capitalism have ditched the Vietnamese to keep down the cost of our holiday petrol, just as we starve the Sri Lanka peasants to keep down the price of our cups of tea.

No, I do not forget the dying bird but I do not enjoy seeing its neck wrung – any more than Tom Paine did when he actually went to France, protested against the murders and was thrown into prison and sentenced to death by his own revolutionary friends. I do not enjoy meeting a man at whose house I have stayed – unshaven and red-eyed with worry over his vanished family. I do not enjoy knowing that one old lady who fed me with great kindness has vowed to swallow cyanide when the communists come. I do not like to recall all those pointless millions of dead, maimed, widowed and orphaned people during the Thirty Years War in this tragic but lovable country.

Spectator, 3 January 1976   *Peter Jenkins*

REACTIONARY CHIC

The Collapse of Democracy by ROBERT MOSS *Temple Smith* £4.95

Death of democracy books are the coming vogue. The spirit of the times is an anxious one and the lead-time of the publishing industry being long, the shock to the western system – which, for convenience, we can date in the autumn of 1973 – is still in the process of being transmitted between hard covers. The thirties were the most prolific period for hard-cover pamphleteering; forebodings about the dictators were amply justified but the democracies emerged victorious and capitalism, for whom the typewriter bells tolled incessantly, not only survived but went on to flourish as never before. The late fifties and early sixties brought another spate of voguish political literature: the what's wrong books boomed; remember *The Stagnant Society*, a paperback best-seller? The literature which accompanied the election of a Labour government in 1964 after thirteen years of Tory rule was harsh in diagnosis but optimistic in prognosis; the spirit of the times was the contagious one of Kennedy's New Frontier and Johnson's Great Society. Now comes the literary backlash against the failure to build Harold Wilson's New Britain while, not only in this country, the depressed spirit of the times is reflected in a new literature of the apocalypse.

Robert Moss's book is not a particularly good one but it has many of the ingredients of a successful vogue book. It has a shrilly arresting title – democracy's 'collapse', is not suffixed with a question mark. The author warns us in an introduction of how 'highly controversial' he is going to be as he sets off, somewhat breathlessly and bossily, to rouse us from our complacent slumbers. One of the tricks of the vogue book trade is to promote some commonplace to the rank of revelation – in this case democracy's tending towards equality at the expense of liberty. Vogue books are usually also eclectic as is this one; from the index, the acknowledgements and references you can see at a glance who's in and who's out and the text is studded with gobbets from more-often-quoted-than-read authors. They do service for argument – as Sir Henry Maine observed . . . as pointed out by von Mises . . . Those two enemies, topicality and profundity, lie down together between the covers of the vogue book and the proofs of this one were updated to take account – as at the middle of this year – of the latest developments in Portugal and in the AEUW elections. A vogue book, above all, must be contemporary – that is to say concerned with the immediate future – while at the same time seeming to be rooted in older, preferably recently rediscovered, truths.

Given the shortcomings of the genre Mr Moss's book is readable and stimulating and not excessively irritating. It is also interesting since it may be an early instance of an unfamiliar phenomenon, a vogue literature of the Right. Mr Patrick Hutber of the *Sunday Telegraph* already has seized joyfully on somebody's reference to the 'trendy right' on the grounds that the Left's best tunes are no longer automatically top of the pops and I suspect that Mr Moss is the harbinger of what we shall soon be sneering at as 'reactionary chic'. The reactionary chic buy their politics at Hayek, shop for economics at the Institute for Economic

Affairs and attend holy worship at the True Church of Milton Friedman. They are for indexing and vouchering, can talk with technical expertise on the subject of counter-insurgency and invest in the fall of the Weimar Republic the same sort of historical and ideological significance which the Left attaches to the Paris Commune.

Mr Moss deserves some welcome – even from nis opponents – as an articulate exponent of right-wing nostrums which, I suspect, are on the way to becoming intellectually fashionable at a popular level. What's wrong with the book is exactly what is wrong with most left wing books of the same ilk: that is that it pounds away at its theme with a hammer steamed by first principles enriched with secondary authorities. The reader should skip Chapter One which is a fictitious 'Letter from London, 1985' derivative of – though not as good as – the setting for Jack London's 'The Iron Heel'. By 1985 Socialism has extinguished liberty and by extrapolation from the imagined future into the real present the 'now' is presented by the author – surely with ludicrous extravagance – as a 'stage of proto-communism'. He refers – as if the point has been demonstrated – to 'what remains of the free society in Britain'.

Starting with what (though he does not attribute it) is Schumpeter's definition of democracy – a mechanism for selecting teams of leaders – Mr Moss asserts (arguing chiefly by quotation from the classics) the classical doctrine that a free market is quintessential to a free society. Who are therefore its enemies? Number One is 'the extraordinary power that is concentrated in the hands of a single social pressure group, the industrial trade unions.' Number Two – although this is not made fully explicit until a later stage in a muddled argument – is 'the absence of constitutional curbs on the power vested in the House of Commons.' In Parliament we see (or so he says) the Party of Equality triumphing over the Party of Liberty: the extinction of liberty and, when it comes to it, equality as well, is 'the alluring horizon towards which Britain is steaming at full speed. . . .'

This is all nonsense and Mr Moss, who has used his eyes and his ears and his common sense as a journalist in Portugal and the Argentine and some other places, clearly hasn't stirred far from his offices in the *Economist* for the purposes of observing his own country. What he has done instead is to bring to bear upon newspaper reports about trade unions and other contemporary domestic problems texts concerned with the age-old tension between democracy and equality. By this means he achieves one of the essential requirements of a vogue book – the perennial made new and urgent.

For a hundred years or more critics of democracy (i.e. representative government elected by universal suffrage) have predicted that liberty will be the inevitable victim of the masses' lust for equality. Because this has so far not proved the case you might think it more worth exploring why than repeating unfulfilled prophecies just as it is more worth explaining the failure of socialism to replace capitalism – except with the aid of arms – than to go on inventing new scenarios for capitalism's inevitable collapse – which is of course another example of how Mr Moss has written an inverted New Left Book.

Mr Moss invests in the unions a mysterious power born of his own ignorance. Trade unions do have too much power but most of it is negative, they constitute one of the most formidable barriers against the advance of equality in what is still a pluralistic system although its structure may be neither to Mr Moss's taste nor mine. Similarly he gets himself into difficulty with his economics – of which he admits knowing little. Having demonstrated by assertion and quotation that a market economy is the precondition of political freedom he is obliged, by circularity of argument, to come down in favour of a market economy. Its performance then becomes a matter of faith. How free a market in order to produce how free a society? He does not discuss.

Indeed the economic section of the book – which is really integral to his whole political and moral argument – is a lamentable example of amateur monetarism and entirely begs the proper subject of his concern, which is the basis of authority in society. For example he makes a point of the difficulty of freezing wages without aid of the army but doesn't see that the same difficulty applies to freezing the money supply. All through the book he talks about 'unions' as if they were simply an unbalancing item in a philosopher's constitution. He doesn't go into 'workers' and work. By what means does he propose to make them work if they won't? At bayonet point? And why if property (Sir Henry Maine *passim*) is synonymous with liberty cannot a job or a work ('restrictive') practice be considered as a form of property and also synonymous with liberty? Democracy has resulted not so much in the expected thrust towards egalitarianism as in a translation of democratic rights into new property rights – jobs, demarcations, tenancies, etc – on a scale inimical not so much to hierarchy but to efficient control – which is another facet of authority.

However a book which raises these and many other questions is worth reading, and Mr Moss should be deplored not for writing it but for his contribution to a growing intellectual fashion which is reactionary in the literal sense of turning to the past in revulsion from the present. If there is a threat to democracy – and, of course, there is if only because there always is, because democracies are ambitious societies prone to dissatisfaction – it stems from the failure of the system to yield the results expected of it, a combination of excessive expectation and under-gratification. The unions – which Mr Moss unthinkingly belabours – are a good example: paradoxically too demanding (powerful?) and too undemanding (feeble?), at the same time a force of radical intent and conservative effect, positive in their tendency at the centre and largely negative at the workplace. British democracy is at risk because of persistent failure but the failure is structural, economic and social. Perhaps the failure is in some way systemic – endemic in our attitudes, habits or institutions – but after reading Mr Moss's book I am not in the least convinced that British democracy is peculiarly vulnerable to self-destruction or that he is entitled, on the evidence he cites, to announce its demise in so voguish and sensational a manner.

Spectator, 20 March 1976　　　　　　　　*Patrick Cosgrave*
THE NICEST PRIME MINISTER

He was expert in all the small things. When advising Mr Edward Heath on how to tackle Mr Wilson at Prime Minister's Question Time (a game which never interested Mr Heath very much, and at which he was, to put it mildly, not very good), Mr John Peyton once drew attention to the studied courtesy with which Mr Wilson treated his backbenchers. He remembered each man's name and constituency; he recalled their special interests and referred to them in his almost invariably lengthy replies; and he always looked over his shoulder at them. Trivial and even minute though all these things were they were essential elements (as Mr Peyton, who understands these matters better than any other senior politician saw) in the make-up of the nicest Prime Minister we have had since Baldwin.

To be sure, towards the end there was a tendency to slip. At the last Labour conference, during the Lucullan festivities arranged by IPL, Mr Wilson appeared to confuse Mr Keith Waterhouse with a senior trade union figure, and made to one the little speech about hobbies and interests that should have been made to the other, and *vice versa*. Throughout his career, however, he has displayed a memory for names, faces and personal concerns equalled only by that very different man, Lord Home. And – with very rare exceptions when he has been over-influenced by the peculiarly harsh personal antagonisms of his personal staff – in nearly all personal dealings he has been the essence of simple straightforwardness.

I propounded the two propositions of the last two paragraphs throughout last Tuesday and, not greatly to my surprise, found them greeted with incomprehension and even anger, especially on the part of Labour MPs. 'What is Harold up to?' was the first reaction of his colleagues, incapable of imagining that the wily Wilson was not using his resignation as part of some devious ploy. And the partisans of Mr Healey, Mr Benn and Mr Jenkins were all convinced that the Prime Minister had behaved with peculiar and special brutality towards their heroes. Even the supporters of Mr Callaghan were at least half-convinced that the reference in the resignation statement to sixty as a suitable age for retirement was a shrewd blow aimed at their sixty-four-year-old candidate.

And – to pile up the evidence against myself – it is fair to say that Mr Wilson has often demonstrated a careful tactical animosity towards some of his senior colleagues. There was a moment, for example, early in the life of the Heath government when Mr Callaghan was being canvassed as a possible replacement for the beaten Wilson. At the time Mr Callaghan was in hospital for an uncomfortable, but far from serious, prostate operation. Mr Wilson arrived late for lunch with some journalists; expatiated on the problems he had had that morning in standing in for Mr Callaghan in confidential discussions with the Government on Northern Ireland; and made sure to leave the impression that, in his view, the Shadow Home Secretary was at death's door. When, before his resignation from the deputy leadership of the Labour party, Mr Roy Jenkins was the darling of the media and Mr Wilson their victim he observed, 'I don't like standing up to my knees in shit while Roy Jenkins rides by on a white charger. I'll have him down in the shit before I finish.' When Mr Benn was scheduled to be chairman of the Labour party conference and looking forward with delight to what seemed a certain personal triumph, Mr Wilson muttered, 'I'll fix him,' and did.

But the method of fixing Mr Benn was peculiarly indicative of the way Mr Wilson played the political game. On the Sunday of the conference he discussed affairs with Mr Jack Jones and some of the senior trade union leaders, thus assuring himself of the support of most of the union block votes. And then, while Mr Benn was fumbling about in the chairmanship, he made a great rabble-rousing speech. There was nothing particularly devious about that; nothing, indeed, exceptional in the way of party management. When he used his prerogative as Leader to deny Mr Callaghan opportunities for personal advancement, or when he immured Mr Jenkins in the sepulchre of the Home Office, he was acting defensively, not offensively. Any colleague damaged by Mr Wilson was a colleague who had first encouraged – or even taken part in – moves against him. Self-preservation, rather than self-advancement, was usually the motive for a Wilsonian intrigue.

And even in the direct and bloody political conflict with leaders of the Conservative party, in the course of which he coined some of the most devastating and hurtful epigrams of recent times (as when he referred to Mr Macmillan, greeting Mr Butler on his return from a trip overseas, as having grasped his colleague warmly – by the throat) there was a curious diffidence. If you watched Mr Wilson carefully in the few seconds following the utterance of one of these savageries you could see a physical recoil from the effect of the words he had spoken. His lower lip would drop, and he would take half a step back from whatever podium he was using.

But he was, nonetheless, a cat. He chuckled for weeks to his intimates about his cleverness in making Mr Jeremy Thorpe a Privy Councillor, thus irritating Mr Heath extremely by the implication that there were two leaders of the opposition. And, in the last days of the Wilson era, he took the greatest pleasure in treating Mr Heath with the utmost courtesy and respect, often wondering aloud how it was that the Conservative party had failed to recognise the merits of so singular a man. By that time, however, the opposition was used to his little stylistic ploys, and refused to rise to the bait. From being feared he was achieving the status of a character.

The mystery about him was the low esteem in which he was held by his own party. So successful a leader – in electoral terms – would have been feted by the Conservatives, but the view of Mr Wilson held by most of his backbenchers was a derisive one. They recognised, rather grudgingly, that he was the only leader likely to be able to hold their motley ranks together, and they loved it when he savaged the political enemy. But from 1966 onwards they were convinced that he was incurably frivolous, and wholly without principle and – since to be a Socialist one must be eternally convinced that governments ought to be doing things of a large but often unspecified character – they therefore continually believed that they deserved better.

That there is an element of frivolity in Mr Wilson's make-up nobody – except possibly the storm troopers of his private office, like Lady Falkender and Mr Joe Haines – could doubt. But it was, if I may so express it, a serious frivolity, the product, in his second period of office, of a curious kind of fatalism. No Prime Minister this century had, on entering office, as many ideological and emotional commitments guaranteed to get him into trouble as Mr Wilson had in 1964. From the commitment to an East of Suez policy to the determination to maintain the fixed parity of the pound the albatrosses round his neck were each heavy and damaging. But when, against his own expectations, he became Prime Minister again in 1974 he was intellectually convinced, as he had emotionally suspected, that policies were irrelevant, and that the old true business of a government was to carry on. For this reason he was unmoved, on Tuesday, by genuinely felt criticisms to the effect that it was irresponsible of him to leave office during a sterling crisis. There are, of course, Trollopian times when the only business of government *is* to exist. It seems unlikely, however, that the historian will judge that the Wilson era was one of them; and his final epitaph is therefore likely to suggest that he was a palliator of crisis, not a man who could solve great problems. He is Labour's Baldwin; and he will, like Baldwin, be remembered as a simple man who became an enigma.